The Cross & The

When Calvary
Becomes
The Nursery

A Journey of Discovery
With Archbishop Fulton J. Sheen

Allan Smith

Bishop Sheen Today

280 John Street Midland, Ontario, Canada L4R 2J5

www.bishopsheentoday.com

Library of Congress Cataloging-in-Publication Data

Names: Sheen, Fulton J. (Fulton John), 1895-1979, author. | Smith, Al (Allan J.), editor. | Sheen, Fulton J. (Fulton John), 1895-1979. Cross and the Beatitudes. | Sheen, Fulton J. (Fulton John), 1895-1979. Rainbow of sorrow. | Sheen, Fulton J. (Fulton John), 1895-1979. Seven last words. | Sheen, Fulton J. (Fulton John), 1895-1979. Seven virtues. | Sheen, Fulton J. (Fulton John), 1895-1979. Seven words of Jesus and Mary. | Sheen, Fulton J. (Fulton John), 1895-1979. Seven words to the Cross. | Sheen, Fulton J. (Fulton John), 1895-1979. Victory over vice. | Sheen, Fulton J. (Fulton John), 1895-1979. Cross and the Beatitudes.

Title: The Cross & The Crib. When Calvary becomes the nursery. A journey of discovery with Archbishop Fulton J. Sheen.

Archbishop Fulton J. Sheen ; compiled by Allan Smith.

Scripture quotations are taken from the Douay-Rheims edition of the Old and New Testaments.

Description: Midland, Ontario: Bishop Sheen Today Publishing, 2021. | Includes bibliographical references.

Identifiers: paperback ISBN 978-1-990427510 /

e-Book ISBN 978-1-990427-03-9

Subjects: LCSH: Jesus Christ — Seven last words.

Scripture quotations are taken from the Douay-Rheims edition of the Old and New Testaments.

To Our Lady, Seat of Wisdom, in humble petition that, through the Immaculate Heart of Mary, the world may find its way back to the Sacred Heart of Jesus

With filial gratitude and affection, I dedicate this publication to these two Holy Hearts, which overflow with love and mercy for all mankind.

Ad maiorem Dei gloriam - (For the greater glory of God)

Reflections that transformed the hearts and minds of millions all over the world, written by Archbishop Fulton J. Sheen, on the seven last words of Christ.

From the central cross on Calvary come the answers for overcoming sin and brokenness. Those who will take these meditations to heart will find hope, healing, and restoration.

Jesus calls all His children to the pulpit of the Cross, and every word He says to them is set down for the purpose of an eternal publication and undying consolation.

There was never a preacher like the dying Christ.

There was never a congregation like that which gathered about the pulpit of the Cross.

And there was never a sermon like the Seven Last Words.

Archbishop Fulton J. Sheen

THE SEVEN LAST WORDS OF CHRIST

The First Word

"Father, Forgive Them For They
Know Not What They Do."

The Second Word

"This Day Thou Shalt Be With Me In Paradise."

The Third Word

"Woman, Behold Thy Son; Behold Thy Mother."

The Fourth Word

"My God! My God!
Why Hast Thou Forsaken Me?"

The Fifth Word

"I Thirst."

The Sixth Word

"It Is Finished."

The Seventh Word

"Father, Into Thy Hands
I Commend My Spirit."

CONTENTS

INTRODUCTION 1
WOMAN BEHOLD THY SON 5
THE VALUE OF IGNORANCE 9
THY KINGDOM COME 19
THE SECRET OF SANCTITY 21
THE SANCTUS 29
THE FELLOWSHIP OF RELIGION 37
BLESSED ARE THE CLEAN OF HEART 47
CONFIDENCE IN VICTORY 55
THE SUFFERING OF THE INNOCENT 67
RELIGION IS A QUEST 77
LUST 85
THE HOUR 95
PRUDENCE 103
THE PURPOSE OF LIFE 113
THE SELFISH 121
WHEN CALVARY BECOMES THE NURSERY . 135
ACKNOWLEDGMENTS 147
ABOUT THE AUTHOR 149
BIBLIOGRAPHY NOTES 155

INTRODUCTION

Archbishop Fulton J. Sheen was a man for all seasons. Over his lifetime he spent himself for souls, transforming lives with the clear teaching of the truths of Christ and His Church through his books, his radio addresses, his lectures, his television series, and his many newspaper columns.

The topics of this much-sought-after lecturer ranged from the social concerns of the day to matters of faith and morals. With an easy and personable manner, Sheen could strike up a conversation on just about any subject, making numerous friends as well as converts.

During the 1930s and '40s, Fulton Sheen was the featured speaker on The Catholic Hour radio broadcast, and millions of listeners heard his radio addresses each week. His topics ranged from politics and the economy to philosophy and man's eternal pursuit of happiness.

Along with his weekly radio program, Sheen wrote dozens of books and pamphlets. One can safely say that through his writings, thousands of people changed their perspectives about God and the Church. Sheen was quoted as saying, "There are not one hundred people in the United States who hate the Catholic Church, but there are millions who hate what they wrongly perceive the Catholic Church to be."

Possessing a burning zeal to dispel the myths about Our Lord and His Church, Sheen gave a series of powerful presentations on Christ's Passion and His seven last words from the Cross. As a Scripture scholar, Archbishop Sheen knew full well the power contained in preaching Christ crucified. With St. Paul, he could say, "For I decided to know nothing among you except Jesus Christ and him crucified" (1 Cor. 2:2).

During his last recorded Good Friday address in 1979, Archbishop Sheen spoke of having given this type of reflection on the subject of Christ's seven last words from the cross "for the fifty-eighth consecutive time." Whether from the young priest in Peoria, Illinois, the university professor in Washington, D.C., or the bishop in New York, Sheen's messages were sure to make an indelible mark on his listeners.

Along with Archbishop Fulton Sheen's great love for preaching about the power of the cross, he professed great love for the Blessed Virgin Mary and often spoke of his devotion to her. As a tribute to the Mother of God, when being consecrated as a Bishop in 1951, he added to his coat of arms the words *'Da Per Matrem Me Venire'*, meaning: *'That I may come to Jesus through His Mother.'*

He wrote many books about the Blessed Virgin Mary including *The Seven Words of Jesus and Mary* (1945) and *The World's First Love* (1952). It seemed that he never missed an opportunity to talk about her and to recommend that his audience goes to her whenever they needed help.

Now for some, entertaining the thought of having the Blessed Virgin Mary as their mother might sound a little far-fetched. Yes, Mary is the biological Mother of Jesus but how could she become anyone else's mother? And how could anyone love this mother that lives in heaven and we cannot see?

For many Catholics all over the world, this tradition of accepting Mary as their mother and trusting in her 'heavenly influence' comes naturally. But for others, including this author, a better explanation would have to be given, before we would be willing to accept such teaching.

Archbishop Fulton J. Sheen was aware of the reservations people had towards the Blessed Virgin Mary. Sheen addressed the prejudices, misconceptions, and the lack of understanding of who the Blessed Mother is during his many radio addresses, lectures and television broadcasts.

In the pages that will follow in this anthology, you will find fifteen short sermons that will take you on a *'journey of discovery'* that will give the reader a new and fresh perspective on the Blessed Virgin Mary and the role she played in salvation history.

These meditations will speak to the Seven Last Words that Jesus spoke from His Cross on Calvary and correlate them to the seven recorded times that the Blessed Virgin Mary spoke in the scriptures. The Words are not necessarily related to all the words she said but they do make convenient points of illustrations.

This book has only one aim: to awaken a love for the Passion of Our Lord Jesus Christ and to incite a greater appreciation for the Blessed Virgin Mary. If it does that in but one soul, its publication has been justified.

WOMAN BEHOLD THY SON

An angel of light went out from the great white Throne of Light and descended over the plains of Esdraelon, past the daughters of the great kingdoms and empires, and came to where a humble virgin of Nazareth knelt in prayer, and said, "Hail, full of grace!" These were not words; they were the Word. "And the Word became flesh." This was the first Annunciation.

Nine months passed and once more an angel from that great white Throne of Light came down to shepherds on Judean hills, teaching them the joy of a "Gloria in Excelsis," and bidding them worship Him Whom the world could not contain, a "Babe wrapped in swaddling clothes and laid in a manger." Eternity became time, Divinity incarnate, God a man; Omnipotence was discovered in bonds. In the language of Saint Luke, Mary "brought forth her first-born Son . . .and laid Him in a manger." This was the first Nativity.

Then came Nazareth and the carpenter shop where one can imagine the Divine Boy, straitened until baptized with a baptism of blood, fashioning a little cross in anticipation of a great Cross that would one day be His on Calvary. One can also imagine Him in the evening of a day of labor at the bench, stretching out His arms in exhausted relaxation, whilst the setting sun traced on the opposite wall the shadow of a man on a cross. One can, too, imagine His Mother seeing in each nail the prophecy and the tell-tale of a day when men would carpenter to a Cross the One who carpentered the universe.

Nazareth passed into Calvary and the nails of the shop into the nails of human malignity. From the Cross, He completed His last will and testament. He had already committed His blood to the Church, His garments to His enemies, a thief to Paradise, and would soon commend His body to the grave and His soul to His Heavenly Father. To whom, then, could He give the two treasures which He loved above all others, Mary and John? He would bequeath them to one another, giving at once a son to His Mother and a Mother to His friend. "Woman!" It was the second Annunciation! The midnight hour, the silent room, the ecstatic prayer had given way to the Mount of Calvary, the darkened sky, and a Son hanging on a Cross. Yet, what consolation! It was only an angel who made the first Annunciation, but it is God's own sweet voice, which makes the second.

"Behold thy son!" It was the second Nativity! Mary had brought forth her First-born without labor, in the cave of Bethlehem; she now brings forth her second-born, John, in the labors of the Cross. At this moment Mary is undergoing the pains of childbirth, not only for her second-born, who is John, but also for the millions who will be born to her in Christian ages as "Children of Mary." Now we can understand why Christ was called "her First-born." It was not because she was to have other children by the blood of flesh, but because she was to have other children by the blood of her heart. Truly, indeed, the Divine condemnation against Eve is now renewed against the new Eve, Mary, for she is bringing forth her children in sorrow.

Mary, then, is not only the Mother of Our Lord and Saviour, Jesus Christ, but she is also our Mother, and this not by a title of courtesy, not by legal fiction, not by a mere figure of speech, but by the right of bringing us forth in sorrow at the foot of the Cross. It was by weakness and disobedience at the foot of the tree of Good and Evil that Eve lost the title, Mother of the Living; it is at the foot of the tree of the Cross that Mary, by sacrifice and obedience, regained for us the title, Mother of Men. What a destiny to have the Mother of God as my Mother and Jesus as my Brother!

PRAYER

O MARY! As Jesus was born to thee in thy first Nativity of the flesh, so we have been born of thee in thy second Nativity of the spirit. Thus thou didst beget us into a new world of spiritual relationship with God as our Father, Jesus as our Brother, and thou as our Mother! If a mother can never forget the child of her womb, then, Mary, thou shalt never forget us. As thou wert Co-Redemptrix in the acquisition of the graces of eternal life, be thou also our Co-Mediatrix in their dispensation. Nothing is impossible for thee, because thou art the Mother of Him who can do all things. If thy Son did not refuse thy request at the banquet of Cana, He will not refuse it at the celestial banquet where thou art crowned as Queen of the Angels and Saints. Intercede therefore to thy Divine Son, that He may change the waters of my weakness into the wine of thy strength. Mary, thou art the Refuge of Sinners! Pray for us, now prostrate at the foot of the Cross. Holy Mary, Mother of God, pray for us sinners, now and at the hour of our death. Amen. (1)

The Seven Last Words, 1933

THE VALUE OF IGNORANCE

The First Word from The Cross

Father, Forgive Them For They Know

Not What They Do. (Luke 23:34)

The Blessed Virgin Mary's Response

How shall this be done, because I know not man? (Luke 1:34)

One thousand years before Our Blessed Lord was born, there lived one of the greatest of all poets: the glorious Homer of the Greeks. Two great epics are ascribed to him: one the Iliad; the other, the Odyssey. The hero of the Iliad was not Achilles, but Hector, the leader of the enemy Trojans whom Achilles defeated and killed. The poem ends not with the glorification of Achilles but of the defeated Hector.

The other poem, the Odyssey, has as its hero, not Odysseus, but Penelope, his wife, who was faithful to him during the years of his travels. As the suitors pressed for her affections, she told them that when she finished weaving the garment they saw before her, she would listen to their courtship. But each night she unraveled what she had woven in the day, and thus remained faithful until her husband returned. "Of all women," she said, "I am the most sorrowful." Well, might be applied to her the words of Shakespeare: "Sorrow sits in my soul as on a throne. Bid kings come and bow down to it."

For a thousand years before the birth of Our Blessed Lord, pagan antiquity resounded with these two stories of the poet who threw into the teeth of history the mysterious challenge of glorifying a defeated man and hailing a sorrowful woman. How, the subsequent centuries asked, could anyone be victorious in defeat and glorious in sorrow? And the answer was never given until that day when there came One Who was glorious in defeat: the Christ on His Cross and one who was magnificent in sorrow: His Blessed Mother beneath the cross.

It is interesting that Our Lord spoke seven times on Calvary and that His Mother is recorded as having spoken but seven times in Sacred Scripture. Her last recorded word was at the Marriage Feast of Cana when her Divine Son began His Public Life. Now that the sun was out, there was no longer need of the moon to shine. Now that the Word has spoken, there was no longer need of words.

St. Luke records five of the seven words which he could have known only from her. St. John records the other two. One wonders, as Our Blessed Lord spoke each of His Seven Words if Our Blessed Mother at the foot of the Cross did not think of each of her corresponding words. Such will be the subject of our meditation: Our Lord's Seven Words on the Cross and the Seven Words of Mary's Life.

Men cannot stand weakness. Men are, in a certain sense, the weaker sex. There is nothing that so much unnerves a man as a woman's tears. Therefore men need the strength and the inspiration of women who do not break down in a crisis. They need someone not prostrate at the foot of the cross, but standing, as Mary stood. John was there; he saw her standing, and he wrote it down in his Gospel.

Generally, when innocent men suffer at the hands of impious judges, their last words are either: "I am innocent" or "The courts are rotten." But here, for the first time in the hearing of the world, is one who asked neither for the forgiveness of His own sins, for He is God, nor proclaimed His own innocence, for men are not judges of God. Rather does He plead for those who kill him: "Father, forgive them, for they know not what they do" *(Luke 23:34)*.

Mary beneath the gibbet heard Her Divine Son speak that First Word. I wonder when she heard him say, "know not" if she did not recall her own First Word. It, too, contained those words: "know not."

The occasion was the Annunciation, the first good news to reach the earth in centuries. The angel announced to her that she was to become the Mother of God: "Behold thou shalt conceive in thy womb and shalt bring forth a son: and thou shalt call his name Jesus. He shall be great and shall be called the son of the Most High. And the Lord God shall give unto him the throne of David, his father: and he shall reign in the house of Jacob forever. And of his Kingdom, there shall be no end. And Mary said to the Angel: How shall this be done because I know not man?" *(Luke 1:31-34)*.

These words of Jesus and Mary seem to suggest that there is sometimes wisdom in not knowing. Ignorance is here represented not as a cure, but a blessing. This rather shocks our modern sensibilities which so much glorify education, but that is because we fail to distinguish between true wisdom and false wisdom. St. Paul called the wisdom of the world "foolishness," and Our Blessed Lord thanked His Heavenly Father that He had not revealed Heavenly Wisdom to the worldly-wise.

The ignorance, which is here extolled, is not ignorance of the truth, but ignorance of evil. Notice it first of all in the word of Our Saviour to His executioners: He implied that they could be forgiven only because they were ignorant of their terrible crime. It was not their wisdom that would save them, but their ignorance.

If they knew what they were doing as they smote the Hands of Everlasting Mercy, dug the Feet of the Good Shepherd, crowned the Head of Wisdom Incarnate, and still went on doing it, they would never have been saved. They would have been damned! It was only their ignorance which brought them within the pale of redemption and forgiveness. As St. Peter told them on Pentecost: "I know that you did it through ignorance: as did also your rulers." *(Acts 3:17).*

Why is it that you and I, for example, can sin a thousand times and be forgiven, and the angels who have sinned but once are eternally unforgiven? The reason is that the angels *knew* what they were doing. The angels see the consequences of each and every one of their decisions with the same clarity that you see that a part can never be greater than the whole. Once you make that judgment, you can never take it back. It is irrevocable; it is eternal.

Now the angels saw the consequences of their choices with still greater clarity. Therefore, when they made a decision, they made it knowingly, and there was no taking it back. They were lost forever. Tremendous are the responsibilities of knowing! Those who know the truth will be judged more severely than those who know it not. As Our Blessed Lord said: "If I had not come...they would not have sin" *(John 15:22).*

The First Word Our Blessed Mother spoke at the Annunciation revealed the same lesson. She said: "I know not man." Why was there a value in not knowing man? Because she had consecrated her virginity to God. At a moment when every woman sought the privilege of being the mother of the Messiah, Mary gave up the hope and received it. She refuses to discuss with an angel any kind of compromise with her high resolve.

If the condition of becoming the Mother of God was the surrender of her vow, she would not make that surrender, knowing man would have been evil for her, though it would not have been evil in other circumstances. Not knowing man is a kind of ignorance, but here it proves to be such a blessing that in an instant the Holy Spirit overshadows her, making her a living ciborium privileged to bear within herself for nine months the Guest Who is the Host of the World.

These first words of Jesus and Mary suggest there is value in not knowing evil. You live in a world in which the worldly-wise says: "You do not know life; you have never lived." They assume that you can know nothing except by experience — experience not only of good but of evil.

It was with this kind of lie that Satan tempted our First Parents. He told them that the reason God forbade them to eat of the tree of the knowledge of good and evil was because God did not want them to be wise as He was wise. Satan did not tell them that if they came to a knowledge of good and evil, it would be very different from God's knowledge.

God knows evil only abstractly, i.e., by negation of His Goodness and Love. But man would know it concretely and experimentally, and thus would to some extent fall captive to the very evil which he experienced. God wanted our First Parents to know typhoid fever, for example, as a healthy doctor knows it; he did not want them to know it as the stricken patient knows it. And from that day of the Great Lie, down to this, no one is better because he knows evil through experience.

Examine your own life. If you know evil by experience, are you wiser because of it? Have you not despised that very evil and are you not the more tragic for having experienced it? You may even have become mastered by the evil you experienced. How often the disillusioned say: "I wish I had never tasted liquor" or "I regret the day I stole my first dollar," and "I wish I had never known that person." How much wiser you would have been had you been ignorant!

Over and over again, when you broke some law which you thought arbitrary and meaningless, you discovered the principle which dictated it. As a child, you could not understand why your parents forbade you to play with matches, but the burn convinced you of the truth of the law. So the world by violating God's moral law is finding through war, strife, and misery the wisdom of the law. How it would now like to unlearn its false learning!

Think not, then, that in order to "know life" you must "experience evil." Is a doctor wiser because he is prostrate with disease? Do we know cleanliness by living in sewers? Do we know education by experiencing stupidity? Do we know peace by fighting? Do we know the joys of vision by being blinded? Do you become a better pianist by hitting the wrong keys? You do not need to get drunk to know what drunkenness is.

Do not excuse yourself by saying, "temptations are too strong" or "good people do not know what temptation is." The good know more about the strength of temptations than those who fall. How do you know how strong the current of a river is? By swimming with the current or by swimming against it? How do you know how strong the enemy is in battle? By being captured or by conquering? How can you know the strength of a temptation unless you overcome it? Our Blessed Lord really understands the power of temptation better than anyone, because He overcame the temptations of Satan.

The great fallacy of modern education is the assumption that the reason there is evil in the world is because there is ignorance, and that if we pour more facts in the minds of the young, we will make them better. If this were true, we should be the most virtuous people in the history of the world, because we are the best educated.

The facts, however, point the other way: Never before has there been so much education and never before so little coming to the knowledge of the truth. We forget that ignorance is better than error. *Scientia* is not *sapientia*. Much of modern education is making the mind sceptical about the wisdom of God. The young are not born sceptics, but a false education can make them sceptical. The modern world is dying of sceptic poisoning.

The fallacy of sex education is assuming that if children know the evil effects of certain acts, they will abstain from those acts. It is argued that if you knew there was typhoid fever in a house, you would not go into that house. But what these educators forget is that sex-appeal is not at all like the typhoid fever appeal. No person has an urge to break down the doors of a typhoid patient, but the same cannot be said about sex. There is a sex-impulse, but there is no typhoid instinct.

Sex wisdom does not necessarily make one wise; it can make one desire the evil, particularly when we learn that the evil effects can be avoided. Sex Hygiene is not morality. Soap is not the same as virtue. Badness comes not from our ignorance of knowing, but from our perversity of doing.

That is why in our Catholic schools, we train and discipline the will as well as inform the intellect because we know that character is in our choices, not in our knowing. All of us already *know* enough to be good, even before we start to school. What we have to learn is how to *do better*.

If we forget the burden of our fallen nature and the accumulated proneness to evil that comes from submitting to it, we soon become chained as Samson was and all the education in the world cannot break those chains. Education may conceivably rationalize the chains and make us believe they are charms, but only the effort of the will plus the grace of God can free us from their servitude. Without those two energies, we will never do one jot or tittle beyond that which we have already done.

Train your children and yourself, then, in the true wisdom which is the knowledge of God, and in the ignorance of the things that are evil. The unknown is the undesired; to be ignorant of wickedness is not to desire it. There are no joys like Innocence.

Here on the Cross and on its shadow were the two most Innocent Persons of all history: Jesus was absolutely sinless because He is the Son of God; Mary was Immaculate because she was preserved free from original sin, in virtue of the merits of her Divine Son. It was their innocence which made their sufferings so keen.

People living in dirt hardly ever realize how dirty dirt is. Those who live in sin hardly understand the horror of sin. The one peculiar and terrifying thing about sin is that the more experience you have with it, the less you know about it. You become so identified with it that you know neither the depths to which you have sunk nor the heights from which you have fallen.

You never know you were asleep until you wake up, and you never know the horror of sin until you get out of sin. Hence, only the sinless really know what sin is. And since here on the Cross and beneath it, there is Innocence at its highest, it follows that there was also the greatest sorrow. Since there was no sin, there was the greatest understanding of its evil. It was their innocence, or their ignorance of evil, which made the agonies of Calvary.

To Jesus Who forgave those who "know not," to Mary who won God because she could say "I know not," pray that you may know not evil and thus be good.

Honestly, if you had the choice now either of learning more about the world or of unlearning the evil you know, would you not rather unlearn than learn? Would you not be better if you were stripped of your wickedness than if you were clothed in the sheepskin of diplomas?

Would you not like to be right now, just as you came from the hands of God at the baptismal font, with no worldly wisdom yet gathered to your mind, so that like an empty chalice, you might spend your life filling it with the wine of His Love? The world would call you ignorant, saying you knew nothing about life. Do not believe it — you would have Life! Therefore you would be one of the wisest persons in the world.

There is so much error in the world today, there are such vast areas of experienced and lived evil, that it would be a blessing if some generous soul would endow a University for Unlearning. Its purpose would be to do with error and evil exactly what doctors do with disease.

Would you be surprised to know that Our Lord did actually institute such a University for Unlearning, and to it, all devout Catholics go about once a month? It is called the confessional! You will not be given a sheepskin when you walk out of that confessional, but you will feel like a lamb because Christ is your Shepherd. You will be amazed at how much you will learn by unlearning. It is easier for God to write on a blank page than on one covered with your scribblings. (2)

The Seven Words of Jesus and Mary, 1945

THY KINGDOM COME

"Thy Kingdom Come"

"Woman, behold thy son."

When Our Lord taught us the "Our Father" He made the third petition a prayer that God's Kingdom, which is the kingdom of saints, might come. Now in His own last prayer, He addresses the saintliest of creatures: John the beloved disciple, and Mary, His Mother. He was dying on the cross for no other reason than to make us saints – and to be a saint means to be fixed in goodness. The saintliest creature God ever made was the Mother of His Divine Son, for she was not only "full of grace" but a co-Redeemer with her Son now suspended above her head. When Our Lord looked down to her and commended her to us in the person of John, saying: "Behold thy mother", He was equivalently telling us: "If you wish to be holy, behold thy mother; if you really wish that My Kingdom will come, then behold thy mother; if you will to be rooted in goodness and be perfect as your heavenly Father is perfect, then behold thy mother".

Our Lord made no exception; His Mother was given to all – to those who sin, to those who mourn, and to those who suffer.

Are you a sinner? Then go to Mary, for She knows something of the bitterness of your soul. Mary knows what it is for a soul to be without Jesus, for during the three days loss she merited to become the Refuge of Sinners. She was meriting the honor anew at this very moment. She would never have been given to sinners had there not been a crucifixion, there never would have been a crucifixion without sin, and there never would have been sin without sinner – and where sinners are, there are we. Mary, therefore, owes the dignity of her title to us, as sinners. Are you a sinner? Then hear her merciful Son lift me from despair with the words: "Behold thy mother."

Are you a mourner? Have you lost a sweet child, a kind father, a loving mother? Then you have lost only part of what you had. But Mary lost everything, for she lost God. To you, who mourn: "Behold thy mother."

In those moments of unbounded grief, when you are oppressed by your sins, and dripping tears from a wounded or broken heart; when you are sick of what you have and hunger after what you have not; when holiness seems such a distant goal and heaven so far off, then say to Mary: "Remember, Jesus, said to thee, concerning me as wicked as I am: 'Woman, behold thy son'." (3)

The Seven Last Words & The Our Father, 1935

THE SECRET OF SANCTITY

The Second Word From The Cross

This Day Thou Shalt Be With Me in Paradise. (Luke 23:43)

The Blessed Virgin Mary's Response

Be it done to me according to thy word.

(Luke 1:38)

THERE IS ONLY ONE thing in the world that is definitely and absolutely your own, and that is your will. Health, power, possessions, and honor can all be snatched from you, but your will is irrevocably your own, even in hell. Hence, nothing really matters in life, except what you do with your will. It is that which makes the story of the two thieves crucified on either side of Our Lord, for here is the drama of wills.

Both thieves at first blasphemed. There was no such thing as the good thief at the beginning of the Crucifixion. But when the thief on the right heard that Man on the Central Cross forgive His executioners, he had a change of soul.

He began to accept his sorrows. He took up his cross as a yoke rather than as a gibbet, abandoned himself to God's Will, and turning to the rebellious thief on the left said: "Neither dost thou fear God, seeing thou art under the same condemnation? And we indeed justly: for we receive the due reward of our deeds. But this man hath done no evil" *(Luke 23:40-41).*

Then from his heart already so full of surrender to His Saviour, there came this plea, "Remember me when thou shalt come into thy kingdom" *(Luke 23:42)*. Immediately there came the answer: "Amen I say to thee: this day thou shalt be with me in paradise" *(Luke 23:43)*.

"Thou." We are all individuals in the sight of God. He called His sheep by name. This word was the foundation of Christian democracy. Every soul is precious in God's sight, even those whom the state casts out and kills.

At the foot of the cross, Mary witnessed the conversion of the good thief, and her soul rejoiced that he had accepted the Will of God. Her Divine Son's second word promising Paradise as a reward for that surrender, reminded her of her own Second Word thirty years before, when the angel had appeared to her and told her that she was to be the Mother of Him Who was now dying on the Cross.

In her First Word, she asked how this would be accomplished since she knew not man. But when the angel said she would conceive of the Holy Spirit, Mary immediately answered: "Be it done to me according to thy word" *Fiat mihi* secundum verbum tuum. *(Luke 1:38)*

This was one of the great Fiats of the world. The first was at Creation when God said: *Fiat Lux*: "Let there be light"; another was in Gethsemani, when the Saviour, pressing the chalice of redemption to his lips, cried: *Fiat voluntas tua*: "Thy will be done" *(Matthew 26:42)*. The third was Mary's, pronounced in a Nazarene cottage, which proved to be a declaration of war against the empire of evil; *Fiat mihi* secundum verbum tuum: "Be it done to me according to thy word" *(Luke 1:38)*.

The Second Word of Jesus on Golgotha and the second Word of Mary in Nazareth teach the same lesson: *Everyone in the world has a cross, but the cross is not the same for any two of us.* The cross of the thief was not the cross of Mary. The difference was due to God's will toward each. The thief was to give life; Mary to accept life. The thief was to hang on his cross; Mary was to stand beneath hers. The thief was to go ahead; Mary to remain behind. The thief received a dismissal; Mary received a mission. The thief was to be received into Paradise, but Paradise was to be received into Mary.

Each of us, too, has a cross. Our Lord said: "If any man will follow me" *(Mark 8:34)*. He did not say: "Take up my cross." My cross is not the same as yours, and yours is not the same as mine. Every cross in the world is tailor-made, custom-built, patterned to fit one and no one else.

That is why we say: "My cross is hard." We assume that other persons crosses are lighter, forgetful that the only reason our cross is hard is simply because it is our own. Our Lord did not make His Cross; it was made for Him. So yours is made by the circumstances of your life, and by your routine duties. That is why it fits so tightly. Crosses are not made by machines.

Our Lord deals separately with each soul. The crown of gold we want may have underneath it the crown of thorns, but the heroes who choose the crown of thorns often find that underneath it is the crown of gold. Even those that seem to be without a cross actually have one.

No one would have ever suspected that when Mary resigned herself to God's Will by accepting the honor of becoming the Mother of God, she would ever have to bear a cross. It would seem, too, that one who was preserved free from original sin should be dispensed from the penalties of that sin, such as pain. Yet this honor brought to her seven crosses and ended by making her the Queen of Martyrs.

There are, therefore, as many kinds of crosses as there are persons: crosses of grief and sorrow crosses of want, crosses of abuse, crosses of wounded love, and crosses of defeat.

There is the cross of widows. How often Our Lord spoke of them, for example, in the parable of the judge and the widow *(Luke 18:1-8)*; when He rebuked the Pharisees who "devour the houses of widows" *(Mark 12:40)*, when he spoke to the widow of Naim *(Luke 7:12)*, and when He praised the widow who threw two mites into the temple treasury *(Mark 12:42)*. Widowhood may have been particularly dear to Him, because His own mother was a widow, for Joseph His foster-father was presumably already dead.

When God takes someone from us, it is always for a good reason. When the sheep have grazed and thinned the grass in the lower regions, the shepherd will take a little lamb in his arms, carry it up the mountain where the grass is green, lay it down, and soon the other sheep will follow. Every now and then Our Lord takes a lamb from the parched field of a family up to those Heavenly Green pastures, so that the rest of the family may keep their eyes on their true home and follow through.

Then there is the cross of sickness, which always has a Divine purpose. Our Blessed Lord said: "This sickness is not unto death, but for the glory of God: that the Son of God may be glorified by it" *(John 11:4)*. Resignation to this particular kind of cross is one of the very highest forms of prayer. Unfortunately, the sick generally want to be doing something else other than the thing that God wants them to do.

The tragedy of this world is not so much the pain in it; the tragedy is that so much of it is wasted. It is only when a log is thrown into the fire that it begins to sing. It was only when the thief was thrown into the fire of a cross that he began to find God. It is only in pain that some begin to discover where Love is.

Because our crosses differ, soul will differ from soul in glory. We think too often that in Heaven there is going to be somewhat the same equality in social positions that we have here; that servants on earth will be servants in heaven; that the important people on earth will be the important people in heaven. This is not true.

God will take into account our crosses. He seemed to suggest that in the parable of Dives and Lazarus: "Son, remember that thou didst receive good things in thy lifetime, and likewise Lazarus evil things: but now he is comforted, and thou art tormented" *(Luke 16:25).*

There will be a bright jewel of merit for those who suffer in this world. Because we live in a world where position is determined economically, we forget that in God's world the royalty are those who do His Will. Heaven will be a complete reversal of values of earth. The first shall be last and the last first, for God is no respecter of persons.

A wealthy and socially important woman went to heaven. St. Peter pointed to a beautiful mansion and said: "This is your chauffeur's home." "Well," said she, "if that is his home, think what mine will be like." Pointing to a tiny cottage, Peter said: "There is yours." "I can't live in that," she answered. And Peter said: "I'm sorry, that is the best I could do with the material you sent me." Those who suffer as the thief did have sent ahead some fine material.

It makes no difference what you do here on earth; what matters is the love with which you do it. The street cleaner who accepts in God's name a cross arising from his state in life, such as the scorn of his fellowmen; the mother who pronounces her *Fiat* to the Divine Will as she raises a family for the Kingdom of God; the afflicted in hospitals who say *Fiat* to their cross of suffering are the uncanonized saints, for what is sanctity but fixation in goodness by abandonment to God's Holy Will?

It is typically American to feel that we are not doing anything unless we are doing something *big*. But from the Christian point of view, there is no one thing that is bigger than any other thing. The bigness comes from the way our wills utilize things. Hence mopping an office for the love of God is bigger than running the office for the love of money.

Most of our misery and unhappiness come from rebellion against our present state coupled with false ambition. We become critical of everyone above us, as if the cloak of honor, which another wears, was stolen from our shoulders. Rest assured that if it is God's Will that we do a certain task, it will be done, though the whole world would rise up and say "Nay." But if we get that honor by the abandonment of truth and humility, it will be bitter as wormwood and as biting as gall.

Each of us is to praise and love God in his own way. The bird praises God by singing, the flower by blooming, the clouds with their rain, the sun with its light, the moon with its reflection, and each of us by the patient resignation to the trials of his state in life.

In what does your life consist except two things? 1) Active duties. 2) Passive circumstances. The first is under your control; these do in God's name. The second is outside your control; these submit to in God's name. Consider only the present; leave the past to God's Justice the future to His Providence. Perfection of personality does not consist in knowing God's plan, but in submitting to it as it reveals itself in the circumstances of life.

There is really one shortcut to sanctity; the one Mary chose in the Visitation, the one Our Lord chose in Gethsemani, the one the thief chose on the Cross — abandonment to the Divine Will.

If the gold in the bowels of the earth did not say *Fiat* to the miner and the goldsmith, it would never become the chalice of the altar. If the pencil did not say *Fiat* to the hand of the writer, we would never have the poem; if Our Lady did not say *Fiat* to the angel, she would never have become the House of Gold; if Our Lord did not say *Fiat* to the Father's Will in Gethsemani, we would never have been redeemed; if the thief did not say *Fiat* in his heart, he never would have been the escort for the Master into Paradise.

The reason most of us are what we are, mediocre Christians, "up" one day, "down" the next, is simply because we refuse to let God work on us. As crude marble, we rebel against the hand of the sculptor; as unvarnished canvas, we shrink from the oils and tints of the Heavenly Artist. We are so "fearful lest having Him we may have nought else beside," forgetful that if we have the fire of Love, why worry about the sparks, and if we have the perfect round, why trouble ourselves with the arc.

We always make the fatal mistake of thinking that it is what we do that matters, when really what matters is what we let God do to us. God sent the angel to Mary, not to ask her to do something, but to let something be done.

Since God is a better artisan than you, the more you abandon yourself to Him, the happier He can make you. It is well to be a self-made man, but it is better to be a God-made man.

God will love you, of course, even though you do not love Him, but remember if you give Him only half your heart, He can make you only fifty percent happy. You have freedom only to give it away. To whom do you give yours? You give it either to the moods of the hour, to your egotism, to creatures or to God.

Do you know that if you give your freedom to God, in heaven, you will have no freedom of choice because once you possess the Perfect, there is nothing left to choose. And still, you will be perfectly free because you will be One with Him Whose Heart is Freedom and Love! (4)

The Seven Words of Jesus and Mary, 1945

THE SANCTUS

"Woman, behold thy son . . . behold thy mother." (John 19:26-27)

Five days ago our Blessed Lord made a triumphal entry into the city of Jerusalem: Triumphant cries rang about His ears; palms dropped beneath His feet, as the air resounded with hosannas to the Son of David and praises to the Holy One of Israel. To those who would have silenced the demonstration in His honor, our Lord reminds them that if their voices were silent, even the very stones would have cried out. That was the birthday of Gothic Cathedrals.

They did not know the real reason why they were calling Him *holy*; they did not even understand why He accepted the tribute of their praise. They thought that they were proclaiming Him a kind of earthly king. But He accepted their demonstration because He was going to be the King of a spiritual empire. He accepted their tributes, their hosannas, their pæans of praise because He was going to His cross as a Victim. And every victim must be holy -- *Sanctus, Sanctus, Sanctus*. Five days later came the *Sanctus* of the Mass of Calvary. But at that *Sanctus* of His Mass, He does not say "holy" -- He speaks *to* the holy ones; He does not whisper "Sanctus" -- He addresses Himself *to* saints, to His sweet Mother Mary, and His beloved disciple, John.

Striking words they are: "Woman, behold thy son . . . behold thy mother." He was speaking now to saints. He had no need of saintly intercession, for He was the Holy One of God. But *we* have need of holiness, for every victim of the Mass must be holy, undefiled, and unpolluted. But how can we be holy participants in the Sacrifice of the Mass? He gave the answer: namely, by putting ourselves under the protection of His Blessed Mother. He addresses the Church and all its members in the person of John, and says to each of us: "Behold thy mother." That is why He addressed her not as "Mother" but as "Woman." She had a universal mission, to be not only His Mother, but to be the Mother of all Christians. She had been His Mother; now she was to be the Mother of His Mystical Body, the Church. And we were to be her children.

There is a tremendous mystery hidden in that one word "Woman." It was really the last lesson in detachment which Jesus had been teaching her these many years, and the first lesson of the new attachment. Our Lord had been gradually "alienating," as it were, His affections from His Mother, not in the sense that she was to love Him less, or that He was to love her less, but only in the sense that she was to love *us more*. She was to be detached from motherhood in the flesh, only to be more attached to that greater motherhood in the spirit. Hence the word: "Woman." She was to make us *other Christs*, for as Mary had raised the Holy One of God, so only she could raise us as holy ones for God, worthy to say *Sanctus, Sanctus, Sanctus*, in the Mass of that prolonged Calvary.

The story of the preparation for her role as Mother of the Mystical Body of Christ is unfolded in three scenes in the life of her divine Son, each one suggesting the lesson which Calvary itself was to reveal: namely, that she was called to be not only the Mother of God, but also the Mother of men: not only the Mother of holiness, but the Mother of those who ask to be holy.

The first scene took place in the Temple where Mary and Joseph found Jesus after a three-day search. The Blessed Mother reminds Him that their hearts were broken with sorrow during the long search, and He answers: "Did you not know that I must be about my Father's business?" Here He was equivalently saying: "I have another business, Mother, than the business of the carpenter shop. My Father has sent Me into this world on the supreme business of Redemption, to make all men adopted sons of My heavenly Father in the greater kingdom of the brotherhood of Christ, Thy Son." How far the full vision of those words dawned upon Mary, we know not; whether she then understood that the Fatherhood of God meant that she was to be the Mother of men, we know not. But certainly, eighteen years later, in the second scene, the marriage feast of Cana, she came to a fuller understanding of that mission.

What a consoling thought it is to think that our Blessed Lord, who talked penance, who preached mortification, who insisted upon taking up the cross daily and following Him, should have begun His public life by assisting at a wedding festival! What a beautiful understanding of our hearts!

When in the course of the banquet the wine was exhausted, Mary, always interested in others, was the first to notice and the first to seek relief from the embarrassment. She simply said to our Blessed Lord, "They have no wine." And our Blessed Lord said to her, "Woman, what is that to me and to thee? my hour is not yet come." "Woman, what is that to me?" He did not call her "Mother," but "Woman" -- the same title she was to receive three years later.

He was equivalently saying to her: "You are asking Me to do something which belongs to Me as the Son of God. You are asking Me to work a miracle which only God can work; you are asking Me to exercise My divinity which has relationship to all mankind, namely as its Redeemer. But once that divinity operates for the salvation of the world, you become not only My Mother, but the Mother of redeemed humanity. Your physical motherhood passes into the wider world of spiritual motherhood, and for that reason I call you: 'Woman.'" And in order to prove that her intercession is powerful in that role of universal motherhood, He ordered the pots filled with water, and in the language of

Crashaw the first miracle was worked: "the conscious waters saw their God and blushed."

The third scene happens within two years. One day as our Lord was preaching someone interrupted His discourse to say, "Thy mother . . . stands without, seeking thee." Our Blessed Lord said, "Who is my mother?" and stretching forth His hands toward His disciples He said: "Behold my mother and my brethren. For whosoever shall do the will of my Father, that is in heaven, he is my brother, and my sister, and mother." The meaning was unmistakable. There is such a thing as spiritual maternity; there are bonds other than those of the flesh; there are ties other than the ties of blood, namely spiritual ties which band together those of the Kingdom where reign the Fatherhood of God and the Brotherhood of Christ.

These three scenes have their climax at the Cross where Mary is called "Woman." It was the second Annunciation. The angel said to her in the first: "Hail, Mary." Her Son speaks to her in the second "Woman." This did not mean she ceased to be His Mother; she is always the Mother of God; but her Motherhood enlarged and expanded; it became spiritual, it became universal, for at that moment she became *our mother*. Our Lord created the bond where it did not exist by nature as only He could do.

And how did she become the Mother of men? By becoming not only the mother, but also the spouse of Christ. He was the new Adam, she is the new Eve. And as Adam and Eve brought forth their natural progeny, which we are, so Christ and His Mother brought forth at the cross their spiritual progeny, which we are: children of Mary, or members of the Mystical Body of Christ. She brought forth her First-born at Bethlehem.

Note that St. Luke calls our Lord the *First-born* -- not that our Blessed Mother was to have other children *according to the flesh*, but only because she was to have other children *according to the spirit*. That moment when our Blessed Lord said to her, "Woman," she became in a certain sense the spouse of Christ and she brought forth in sorrow her first-born in the spirit, and his name was John. Who the second-born was we know not. It might have been Peter. It might have been Andrew. But we at any rate are the millionth-and-millionth-born of that woman at the foot of the Cross. It was a poor exchange indeed, receiving the son of Zebedee in place of the Son of God. But surely our gain was greater, for while she acquired but undutiful and often rebellious children, we obtained the most loving Mother in the world -- the Mother of Jesus.

We are children of Mary -- literally, *children*. She is our Mother, not by title of fiction, not by title of courtesy; she is our Mother because she endured at that particular moment the pains of childbirth for all of us. And why did our Lord give her to us as Mother? Because He knew *we could never be holy without her*. He came to us through her purity, and only through her purity can we go back to her. There is no *Sanctus* apart from Mary. Every victim that mounts that altar under the species of bread and wine, must have said the Confiteor, and become a holy victim -- but there is no holiness without Mary.

Note that when that word was spoken to our Blessed Mother, there was another woman there who was prostrate. Have you ever remarked that practically every traditional representation of the Crucifixion always pictures Magdalene on her knees at the foot of the crucifix? But you have never yet seen an image of the Blessed Mother prostrate. John was there and he tells in his Gospel that she stood. He saw her stand. But why did she stand? She stood to be of service to us. She stood to be our minister, our Mother.

If Mary could have prostrated herself at that moment as Magdalene did, if she could have only wept, her sorrow would have had an outlet. The sorrow that cries is never the sorrow that breaks the heart. It is the heart that can find no outlet in the fountain of tears which cracks; it is the heart that cannot have an emotional break-down that breaks. And all that sorrow was part of our purchase price paid by our Co-Redemptrix, Mary the Mother of God!

Because our Lord willed her to us as our Mother, He left her on this earth after He ascended into heaven, in order that she might mother the infant Church. The infant Church had need of a mother, just as the infant Christ. She had to remain on earth until her family had grown. That is why we find her on Pentecost abiding in prayer with the Apostles, awaiting the descent of the Holy Ghost. She was mothering the Mystical Body of Christ.

Now she is crowned in heaven as Queen of Angels and Saints, turning heaven into another marriage feast of Cana when she intercedes with her divine Saviour in behalf of us, her other children, brothers of Christ and sons of the heavenly Father.

Virgin Mother! What a beautiful conjunction of virginity and motherhood, one supplying the defect of the other. Virginity alone lacks something: there is an incompleteness about it; something unfulfilled; a faculty unused. Motherhood alone loses something: there is a surrender, an unflowering, a plucking of a blossom. Oh! For a *rapprochement* in which there would be a virginity that never lacked anything, and a motherhood that never lost anything! We have both in Mary, the Virgin Mother: Virgin by the overshadowing of the Holy Spirit in Bethlehem and Pentecost; Mother by the millions of her progeny from Jesus unto you and me.

There is no question here of confusing our Lady and our Lord; we venerate our Mother, we worship our Lord. We ask of Jesus those things which only God can give: mercy, grace, forgiveness. We ask that Mary should intercede for us with Him, and especially at the hour of our death. Because of her nearness to Jesus which her vocation involves, we know our Lord listens especially to her appeal. To no other saint can we speak as a child to its mother: no other virgin, or martyr, or mother, or confessor has ever suffered as much for us as she has; no one has ever established better claim to our love and patronage than she.

As the Mediatrix of all graces, all favors come to us from Jesus through her, as Jesus himself came to us through her. We wish to be holy, but we know there is no holiness without her, for she was the gift of Jesus to us at the *Sanctus* of His Cross. No woman can ever forget the child of her womb; then certainly Mary can never forget us. That is why we feel way down deep in our hearts that every time she sees another innocent child at the First Communion rail, or another penitent sinner making his way to the Cross, or another broken heart pleading that the water of a wasted life be changed into the wine of God's love, that she hears once again that word: "Woman, behold thy son." (5)

Calvary and the Mass, 1936

THE FELLOWSHIP OF RELIGION

The Third Word from The Cross

Woman, Behold Thy Son; Behold Thy Mother. (John 19:26, 27)

The Blessed Virgin Mary's Response

And Mary rising up in those days, went into the hill country with haste into a city of Judah. And she entered into the house of Zachary, and saluted Elizabeth. (Luke 1:39, 40)

HAVE YOU EVER SAID, in order to justify your selfishness, "After all, I have my own life to live?" The truth is you have not your own life to live because you have to live it with everyone else. Religion is not what you do with your solitariness, but what you do with your relationships. You were born out of the womb of society, and hence the love of neighbor is inseparable from love of God. "If any man say: I love God, and hateth his brother; he is a liar. For he that loveth not his brother whom he seeth, how can he love God whom he seeth not? "*(1 John 4:20).*

As danger multiplies, human solidarity becomes more evident. Human beings are closer to one another morally in a bomb shelter or shell-hole than they are in a brokerage office or at a bridge table. As sorrow increases, a sense of unity deepens. It is, therefore, only natural to suspect that the peak of tragedy in the lives of our Divine Lord and His Mother on Calvary should best reveal the communal character of religion.

It is particularly interesting to note that the Word Our Lord spoke to His Mother from the Cross is prefaced by St. John, in His Gospel, speaking of the seamless garment which had been worn by our Blessed Lord and for which the soldiers were now shaking dice. "The soldiers, therefore, when they had crucified him, took his garments, (and they made four parts, to every soldier a part) and also his coat. Now the coat was without seam, woven from the top throughout" *(John 19:23)*.

Why, out of all the details of the Passion, should he suddenly begin thinking about a robe? Because it was woven by Mary's hands. It was such a beautiful robe that these hardened criminals refused to tear it apart. Custom gave them the right to the perquisites of those whom they crucified. But here the criminals refused to divide the spoils. They shook dice for it so that the winner had the whole robe.

After having yielded up His garments to those who shook dice for them, He on the Cross now yields up her who wove the seamless garment. Our Blessed Lord looks down to the two most beloved creatures He has on earth: Mary and John. He speaks first to His Blessed Mother. He does not call her "Mother," but "Woman."

As St. Bernard so lovingly put it, if He had called her "Mother," she would have been just His mother and no one else's. In order to indicate that she is now becoming the Mother of all men whom He redeems, He endows her with the title of universal motherhood: "Woman." Then indicating with a gesture of His head the presence of His beloved disciple, He added: "Behold thy son." He does not call him John, for if He did, John would have been only the son of Zebedee; he left him unnamed that he might stand for all humanity.

Our Lord was equivalently saying to His Mother: "You already have one Son and I am He. You cannot have another. All the other sons will be in Me as the branches are in the vine. John is one in Me and I in him. Hence I say not: 'Behold another son!' but 'Behold Me in John and John in Me.' "

It was a kind of testament. At the Last Supper, He willed to mankind His Body and Blood. "This is my body! This is my blood!" Now He was willing His Mother: "Behold thy Mother." Our Blessed Lord was here establishing a new relationship; a relationship by which His own Mother became the mother of all mankind, and we, in turn, became her children.

This new bond was not carnal, but spiritual. There are other ties than those of blood. Blood may be thicker than water, but Spirit is thicker than blood. All men, whatever be their color, race, blood, are one in the Spirit: "For whosoever shall do the will of my Father, that is in heaven, he is my brother, and sister, and mother" *(Matthew 12:50)*.

Mary had seen God in Christ; now her Son was telling her to see her Christ in all Christians. She was never to love anyone else but Him, but He would now be in those whom He redeemed. The night before He had prayed that all men might be one in Him, as there is but one life for the Vine and its branches. Now He was making her the custodian not only of the Vine but also of the branches through time and eternity. She had given birth to the King; now she was begetting the Kingdom.

The very thought of this Bride of the Spirit becoming the Mother of humanity is overwhelming, not because God thought of it, but because we so seldom ever think of it. We have become so used to seeing the Madonna with the Child in Bethlehem that we forget that same Madonna is holding you and me at Calvary.

At the manger, Christ was only a Babe; at Calvary, Christ was the head of redeemed humanity. At Bethlehem, she was the mother of Christ; on Calvary, she became the Mother of Christians. In the stable, she brought forth her Son without pain and became the Mother of Joy; at the Cross, she brought us forth in pain and became the Queen of Martyrs. In neither case shall a woman forget the child of her womb.

When Mary heard Our Blessed Lord establish this new relationship, she remembered so well when this spiritual fellowship began. Her third word, as His, was about the relationship. It was a long time ago.

After the angel announced to her that she was to be the Mother of God, which alone would have bound her to all humanity, the angel added that her elderly cousin, Elizabeth, was now with child: "And behold thy cousin Elizabeth, she also hath conceived a son in her old age: and this is the sixth month with her that is called barren. Because no word shall be impossible with God. And Mary said: Behold the handmaid of the Lord: be it done to me according to thy word. And the angel departed from her."

"And Mary rising up in those days, went into the hill country with haste into a city of Juda. And she entered into the house of Zachary and saluted Elizabeth. And it came to pass that when Elizabeth heard the salutation of Mary, the infant leaped in her womb. And Elizabeth was filled with the Holy Ghost. And she cried out with a loud voice and said: Blessed art thou among women and blessed is the fruit of thy womb. And whence is this to me that the mother of my Lord should come to me? For behold as soon as the voice of thy salutation sounded in my ears, the infant in my womb leaped for joy. And blessed art thou that hast believed because those things shall be accomplished that were spoken to thee by the Lord" (*Luke 1:36-45*).

It is rightly assumed that no one may more justly claim immunity from service to others than a woman bearing a child. If one adds to this, *noblesse oblige*, the fact that this Woman bears within herself the very Lord of the Universe, then of all creatures she might rightfully claim dispensation from social bonds and duties to neighbor. Women in that condition come not to minister but to be ministered unto.

Here we have the spectacle of the greatest of all women becoming the servant of others. Not standing on her dignity saying, "I am the Mother of God," but recognizing the need of her aged cousin, this pregnant Queen, instead of awaiting her hour in isolation *as* other women, mounts a donkey, makes a five-day journey over hill country, and with such a consciousness of spiritual fellowship that she does it, in the language of sacred Scripture, "with haste" *(Luke 1:39)*.

Thirty-three years before Calvary, Mary recognizes that her mission is to bring her Lord to humanity; and with such a holy impatience is she filled that she begins it before her Son has seen the light of day. I love to think of her on this journey as the first Christian Nurse whose service to neighbor is inseparable from bringing Christ into the life of her patient.

There is no record of the exact words that Mary spoke. The Evangelist merely tells us that she saluted Elizabeth. But notice that just as soon as she saluted her cousin, new relationships were immediately established. Elizabeth no longer addresses her as cousin. She says,

"Whence is this to me, that the mother of my Lord should come to me?" *(Luke 1:43).*

Mary is now not just a relative or another mother of another child. She is called the "Mother of God!" But that was not the end of the relationship. Elizabeth's own child in her womb, who was to be called later by the Child in Mary's womb "the greatest man ever born of woman," now stirs in His mother's womb; we might almost say he danced to his birth in salutation to the King of Kings! Two unborn children establish a relationship before either had swung open the portals of flesh.

Notice how much Our Blessed Lady is made the link of bringing Christ to humanity. First of all, it was through her as a Gate of Heaven that He walked into this earth. It was in her as a Mirror of Justice that He first saw with human eyes the reflection of the world He had made. It is in her as a kind of living ciborium that He is carried to the First Communion rail of her cousin's home, where an unborn babe salutes Him as the Host who is to be the Guest of the world. It is through her intercession at Cana that He brings His Divine Power to supply a human need. And it is finally at the Cross that she who gave Christ to the world now receives Him back again in us who have the high and undeserved honor to call ourselves Christian.

Because of this intimacy, I wonder if it is not true that as the world loses veneration for Christ's mother, it loses also its adoration of Christ. Is it not true in earthly relationships that, as a so-called friend ignores your mother when he comes to your home, sooner or later he will ignore you? Conversely, as the world begins knocking at Mary's door, it will find that Our Lord Himself will answer.

If you have never before prayed to Mary, do so now. Can you not see that if Christ Himself willed to be physically formed in her for nine months and then be spiritually formed by her for thirty years, it is to her that we must go to learn how to have Christ formed in us? Only she who raised Christ can raise a Christian.

To develop that spiritual comradeship with Jesus and Mary, the Rosary is most effective. The word, Rosary, means a "garland of roses" culled from the Garden of Prayer. Each decade requires only between two and three minutes; thus the whole Rosary requires only a little over ten minutes.

If you do not say it all at once and on your knees, then say one decade when you arise in the morning, another decade on your way to work, another decade as you sweep the house or wait for your check at the noon lunch hour, another decade just before you go to bed; the last decade you can say in bed just before falling off to sleep.

When you are under twenty-five, you have time for only one decade before falling to sleep; when you get to be forty, you will have time for two; and when you are sixty, you will have time for a dozen.

Because the "Hail Mary" is said many times in the course of a Rosary, do not think of it as a sterile repetition, because each time it is said in a different setting or scene as you meditate, for example, on such mysteries as the Birth of Our Lord, the Crucifixion, the Resurrection, etc. You never thought as a child when you told your mother you loved her that it had the same meaning as it did the last time you told her. Because the background of the affection changed, its affirmation was new. It is the same sun that rises each morning, but it makes a new day.

What are some of the advantages of the Rosary?

1. If you say the Rosary devoutly, and all that it implies every day of your life, you will never lose your soul.

2. If you wish for peace in your heart and in your family and an abundance of heavenly gifts on your household, then assemble your family each night and say the Rosary.

3. If you are anxious to convert a soul to the fullness of God's Love and Life, teach that person to say the Rosary. That person will either stop saying the Rosary, or he will receive the gift of Faith.

4. If a sufficient army of us said the Rosary every day, the Blessed Mother would now, as in the past, obtain from Her Divine Son the stilling of the present tempests, the defeat of the enemies of human civilization, and a real peace in the hearts of tired and straying men.

5. If the cooling of your charity has made you unhappy on the inside and critical of others, then the Rosary, through meditation on Our Lord's great love for you on the Cross and your Mother's affection for you on Calvary, will rekindle your love of God and of neighbor and restore you to a peace which surpasses all understanding.

Do not think that in honoring Our Lady with the Rosary you are neglecting Our Lord. Did you ever know anyone who ignored you by being kind to your mother? If Our Lord said to you "Behold Thy Mother," it well behooves us to respect her whom Our Lord chose above all the creatures of earth. In any case remember, even though you wanted to, you could not stop with her. As Francis Thompson put it:

> The celestial Temptress play,
>
> And all mankind to bliss betray;
>
> With sacrosanct cajoleries
>
> And starry treachery of your eyes,
>
> Tempt us back to Paradise! (6)

The Seven Words of Jesus and Mary, 1945

BLESSED ARE THE CLEAN OF HEART

"Blessed are the clean of heart:

for they shall see God."

"(Son) behold thy mother,

Woman, behold thy son."

On the hill of the Beatitudes, at the beginning of His public life, Our Lord preached: "Blessed are the clean of heart, for they shall see God." Now at the end of His life, on the Hill of Calvary, He speaks to the clean of heart: "(Son) behold your mother, Woman, behold your son."

This, of course, is not the beatitude of the world. The world is living today in what might be described as an era of carnality, which glorifies sex, hates restraint, identifies purity with coldness, innocence with ignorance, and turns men and women into Buddhas with their eyes closed, hands folded across their breasts, intently looking inward, thinking only of self.

It is just precisely against such a glorification of sex, and such egocentrism which is so characteristic of the flesh, that Our Lord reacted in His third Beatitude: "Blessed are the clean of heart."

The third Beatitude and the Third Word are related as theory to practice and as doctrine to example, for it was the purity of Our Lord that made the gift of his Mother possible. This is the one supreme lesson to be drawn from this word, namely, that Mary became Our Mother because her Divine Son was Purity itself. On no other condition could He have given her to us so completely and whole-heartedly.

In order to understand how Mary became Our Mother through purity, dwell for a moment on the nature of flesh. Flesh is essentially selfish even in its legitimate satisfaction. All its pleasures look to itself and not to another. Even the law of self-preservation implies, as the word itself states, a kind of selfishness. In its illegitimate pursuits, flesh is even more selfish still, for to satisfy itself it must tyrannize over others, and consume them to enkindle its own fires.

But God in his wisdom has instituted two escapes from the selfishness of the flesh: the Sacrament of Matrimony and the vow of chastity. Each not only breaks the circle of selfishness but makes possible a greater and wider field of service. Or to turn the truth around: the greater the purity of heart, the less the selfishness.

The first escape from the selfishness of the flesh, which God has instituted, is the Sacrament of Matrimony. Matrimony crushes selfishness, first of all, because it merges individuals into a corporate life in which neither lives for self but for the other; it crushes selfishness also because the very permanence of marriage is destructive of those fleeting infatuations, which are born with the moment and die with it it destroys selfishness, furthermore, because the mutual love of husband and wife takes them out of themselves into the incarnation of their mutual love, their other selves, their children; and finally it narrows selfishness because the rearing of children demands sacrifice, without which, like unwatered flowers, they wilt and die.

But these are only negative aspects of Matrimony in relation to the flesh. What is more important to note is that matrimony cures selfishness by calling the flesh to the service of others. New horizons and vistas of devotion and sacrifice are opened to the eyes of flesh; others become more important than self; the ego becomes less circumscribed and more expansive. If reaches out to others, at times even forgetting self.

And so true is this that there is generally less selfishness in large families than in small. A husband and wife may live only for one another, but a father and mother must die to themselves in order to live for their offspring. All unregulated and egotistic attachments which destroy the integrity of a common life are left behind them. Where their heart is, there is their treasure also. They lay their flesh on the altar of sacrifice that others may live, and this is the beginning of love.

But God has provided still another escape from the selfishness of flesh, one more complete than the Sacrament of Matrimony, and that is the vow of chastity. The man or woman who takes this vow does so, not to escape the sacrifices which marriage demands, but to detach himself from all the ties of the flesh, in order that he may be free for greater service.

As St. Paul puts it: "He that is with a wife is solicitous for the things of the world, how he may please his wife; and he is divided. He that is without a wife is solicitous for the things that belong to the Lord, how he may please God."

The vow is a higher form of sacrifice than matrimony, simply because it purchases greater release from the claims of the flesh. The greater the purity the less the selfishness. He or she who takes it may be free to serve and love not just another man or woman and a few children, but all men and all women and all children in the bonds of charity in Christ Jesus Our Lord.

Marriage releases the flesh from its individual selfishness for the service of the family; the vow of chastity releases the flesh not only from the narrow and circumscribed family where there can still be selfishness, but also for the service of that family which embraces all humanity. That is why the Church asks those who consecrate themselves to the redemption of the world to take a vow and to surrender all selfishness, that they may belong to no one family and yet belong to all.

That is why in that larger family of the Kingdom of God, the priest is called "Father" -- because he has begotten children not in the flesh, but in the spirit. That is why the superior of a religious community of women is called "Mother" -- she has her little flock in Christ. That too is why certain teaching orders of men are called "Brothers," and why women bound in religious life by the vow of chastity are called "Sisters."

They are all one family in which new relations have been established, not by their birth in the flesh but by their birth in Christ -- all selflessly seeking the glory of God and the salvation of sinners, under the one whom they love most on earth: their Holy Father, the successor of Peter, the Vicar of Jesus Christ.

Now if matrimony and the vow of chastity provide releases from the selfishness of the flesh, and if increasing purity prepares for a wider service of others, then what should we expect when we meet perfect purity?

If a person becomes less and less egocentric as he becomes more pure, then what should we look for in perfect sinlessness and perfect purity? If greater purity means greater selflessness, then what should we expect of innocence? The answer is: perfect sacrifice.

Given a character in whom there is no selfishness, either for his own comfort or even for his own life, and you have the sacrifice of the Cross. "For greater love than this no man hath, that a man lay down his life for his friends." Given a purity that rises above all family ties and bonds of blood, and then, as Our Lord told us: "He that doth the will of the Father in heaven is a father, a mother, a brother, and a sister."

Given a purity that is the Purity of Our Lord on the Cross, and you have someone so detached from the ego, so strange to selfishness, so thoughtless of the flesh that He looks upon His Mother, not *uniquely* as His own, but as the Mother of us all. Perfect Purity is perfect selflessness. That is why Christ gives His Mother to us, as represented in the person of John: "Behold thy mother."

He would not be selfish about her; he would not keep just for himself the loveliest and most beautiful of all mothers; He would share His own mother with us: and so at the foot of the Cross He gave her who is the Mother of God to us as the mother of men. No human person could do that because the ties of flesh and the selfishness of the flesh are too close. The flesh is too close to us to enable us to share our mother with others. But absolute purity can.

That is why the Beatitude of Purity is one with the Third Word, where selflessness, reaching its perfection in Purity, gave His life that we might be saved, and gave us His Mother that we might not be orphans.

Purity, then, is not something negative; it is not just an unopened bud; it is not something cold; it is not ignorance of life. Is justice merely the absence of dishonesty? Is mercy merely the absence of cruelty? Is faith merely the absence of doubt? Purity is not merely the absence of sensuality; it is selflessness born of love and the highest love of all.

Everyone with a vow is in love, but not in love with that which dies, but with that love which is eternal -- the love of God. There is a passion about chastity -- what Thompson calls a "passionless passion and wild tranquility."

Chastity is not an impossible virtue. Even those who have it not, may yet possess it. St. Augustine calls Mary Magdalen "the arch-virgin." Think of it! the "arch-virgin." He puts her next to the Blessed Mother in virginity; Magdalen, this common prostitute of the streets! She recovered purity, we might almost say, by receiving in anticipation of the Eucharist, the night she bathed the Feet of Our Lord with tears.

That day she came in contact with purity, and she so lived out its implications that within a short time we find her at the foot of the Cross on Good Friday. But who stands beside her? It is no other than the Blessed Mother.

What a remarkable companionship! a woman whose name a few months ago was synonymous with sin, and the Blessed Virgin! If Mary loved Magdalen, then why cannot she love us? If there was hope for Magdalen, then there can be hope for us. If she recovered purity, then it can be recovered by us. But how, except through Mary, for why is she called Mother Most Pure except to make us pure?

Everyone can go to Mary, not only converted sinners like Magdalen, but holy virgins and good mothers, for she is both Virgin and Mother. Virginity alone seems to lack something. There is a natural incompleteness about it -- a faculty unused. Motherhood alone seems to have lost something. There is something surrendered in motherhood. But in Mary there is "neither lack nor loss". ** There is Virginity and Motherhood -- "springtime of eternal May."

** (Sheila Kay Smith)

Purity, then, is not selfishness; it is surrender, it is thoughtfulness of others, it is sacrifice. It can even reach a peak where the Mother of Jesus can become our mother. Away then with that false maxim of the world which tells us that love is blind. It cannot be blind. Our Lord says it is not blind. "Blessed are the clean of heart, for they shall *see*" -- see even God. Mary, open our eyes! (7)

The Cross and the Beatitudes, 1937

CONFIDENCE IN VICTORY

The Fourth Word from The Cross

My God! My God! Why Hast Thou Forsaken Me? (Mark 15:34)

The Blessed Virgin Mary's Response

My soul doth magnify the Lord. And my spirit hath rejoiced in God my Saviour. Because he hath regarded the humility of his handmaid; for behold from henceforth all generations shall call me blessed. Because he that is mighty, hath done great things to me; and holy is his name. And his mercy is from generation unto generations, to them that fear him. He hath shown might in his arm: he hath scattered the proud in the conceit of their heart. He hath put down the mighty from their seat, and hath exalted the humble. He hath filled the hungry with good things; and the rich he hath sent empty away. He hath received Israel his servant, being mindful of his mercy: As he spoke to our fathers, to Abraham and to his seed forever.
(Luke 1:46-55)

PERHAPS AT NO TIME in modern history was there ever such a flight from life as at the present day. In much modern literature, this is manifested either by a return to the primitive through sex or through the subconscious.

In daily life, too, there is the flight from consciousness through alcoholism, or the flight from decision through indifference, or the flight from freedom by the denial of responsibility. All these are symptoms of despair. Many people, as a result, are cracking up, emotionally, mentally, and morally. Our problem is not to diagnose the malady, but to heal it.

Is there another way out, even in these dark days? For an answer, one must go back to the darkest day the world ever saw, the day when the sun hid its face at noon, as if ashamed to shed its light on the crime men committed at Calvary. It recalled the dark moment of the Old Law when the High Priest, clothed not in gorgeous golden robes, but in simple white, entered into the darkness of the Holy of Holies, to sprinkle it with blood in atonement for the sins of the people. The people could not see him, nor could they hear him. They only knew that his being there was a matter of supreme importance, for not until he emerged might they feel that the weight of their sins had been lifted.

One day that symbol became a reality as darkness spread over the earth, blurring three crosses silhouetted against a black horizon. The True High Priest, clothed in Innocence entered into that place where God had hidden Himself because of man's sins, to sprinkle the Holy of Holies with His own Blood in reparation for the sins of men. We see nothing; there is only an awful silence, a thick gloom, relieved by one cry, sent up from a broken heart of self-abasement: "My God, My God, Why hast thou forsaken me?" *(Mark 15:34)*.

These words were the first words of the prophetic Psalm 21, written 1000 years before this black day. Though the Psalm begins with sadness, it ends with joy, victory, and the assurance of spiritual sovereignty over the earth.

First, there is sorrow:

“O God, my God, look upon me: Why hast thou forsaken me?

"But I am a worm and no man: the reproach of men and the outcast of the people.

"All they that saw me have laughed me to scorn: they have spoken with the lips and wagged the head.

"He hoped in the Lord, let him deliver him: let him save him, seeing he delighted in him.

"They have dug my hands and feet. They have numbered all my bones.

"And they have looked and stared upon me. They parted my garments amongst them: and upon my vesture they cast lots.

Then comes the promise of victory:

"Ye that fear the Lord praise him: all ye the seed of Jacob, glorify him.

"Let all the seed of Israel fear him: because he hath not slighted nor despised the supplication of the poor man.

"Neither hath he turned away his face from me: and when I cried to him, he heard me.

"The poor shall eat and shall be filled: and they shall praise the Lord that seek him: their hearts shall live forever and ever.

“All the ends of the earth shall remember, and shall be converted to the Lord: And all the kindreds of the Gentiles shall adore in his sight.

“For the kingdom is the Lord's, and he shall have dominion over the nations.”

(Psalm 21:1-29)

Mary standing at the foot of the Cross knew her scriptures well. When she heard Our Lord begin Psalm 21, it reminded her of a song that she sang too. It was her fourth Word which she chanted in the home of Elizabeth, the greatest song ever written, "The Magnificat": "My soul doth magnify my Lord." It contains very much the same sentiments of Psalm 21, namely, the assurance of victory.

And Mary said: "My soul doth magnify the Lord. And my spirit hath rejoiced in God my Saviour. Because he hath regarded the humility of his handmaid: for behold from henceforth all generations shall call me blessed. Because he that is mighty hath done great things to me: and holy is his name. And his mercy is from generation unto generations, to them that fear him. He hath showed might in his arm: he hath scattered the proud in the conceit of their heart. He hath put down the mighty from their seat and hath exalted the humble. He hath filled the hungry with good things: and the rich he hath sent empty away. He hath received Israel his servant, being mindful of his mercy. As he spoke to our fathers: to Abraham and to his seed forever" *(Luke 1:46-55)*.

There is something common to both these songs: both were spoken before there was any assurance of victory. In His fourth word from the Cross, the suffering figure looks forward through the darkness to the triumph of the Resurrection, and His spiritual dominion over the earth. In her fourth Word, the Woman, nine months before her child is born, looks down the long procession of the coming ages, and proclaims that when the world's great women like Livia, Julia, and Octavia shall have been forgotten, the ordinary law of human oblivion will be suspended in her favor, because she is the Mother of Him Whose Name is Holy, and Whose Cross is the Redemption of men.

How hopeless from a human point of view was the prospect of a Man of the Cross crying to God in darkness, ever exercising dominion over the earth that rejected Him! How hopeless from a human point of view was the prospect of an insignificant village maiden begetting a Son Who would be the Supreme Revolutionist of the centuries, exalting the poor to the family of the Godhead!

Both were really words of triumph, one of Victory before the battle was over, one of Overlordship before the Lord was born. To both Jesus and Mary, there were treasures in darkness, whether the darkness be on a black hill or in a dark womb.

Are you in the valley of despair? Then learn that the Gospel of Christ can be heard as Good News even by those whose life has been shattered by Bad News, for only those who walk in darkness ever see the stars.

All trusting implies something you cannot see. If you could see, there would be no occasion for trust. When you say you trust a man only insofar as you can see him, you do not trust him at all. Now to trust God means to hold fast to the truth that His purposes are good and holy, not because you see them, but in spite of appearances to the contrary.

The reason, therefore, why some souls emerge purified from catastrophe while other souls come out worse, is because the first had One in Whom they could trust and the second had none but themselves. The atheist, therefore, is properly defined as the person who has no invisible means of support.

Have you ever noticed, as you talk to your fellowmen, the difference in the reaction to crisis on the part of those who have faith in God and His purposes and of those who have not? The man without faith was generally greatly surprised at the dark turn of events with two world wars in twenty-one years, the resurgence of barbarism and the abandonment of moral principles. But the man with faith in God was not so surprised. The sum came out just as he had expected; chaos was in the cards though they had not yet been dealt, for he knew that "unless the Lord build the house, they labor in vain that build it" *(Psalm 126:1)*.

Have you also observed that the person without faith finding his world of "progress" becoming so unprogressive, often reacted by blaming religion, by criticizing the Church, and even by blaspheming God for not stopping the war? Such egotists have some sense of justice, and since they refuse to blame themselves, then they must find a scapegoat.

But the man with faith, in the midst of taunts like that which came from the haughty monarch, "Who is the God that shall deliver you out of my hand" *(Daniel 3:15)*, answers as did the three youths in the fiery furnace: "For behold our God, whom we worship, is able to save us from the furnace of burning fire and to deliver us out of thy hands, O king. But if he will not, be it known to thee, O king, that we will not worship thy gods nor adore the golden statue which thou hast set up" *(Daniel 3:17-18)*. "Although he should kill me, I will trust in him" *(Job 13:15)*.

To bring out this difference between those who can call on God in darkness and those who do not, let us set in contrast a typical modern without faith, and a saint. As an example of the first take H. G. Wells who, for decades, hoped that "man with his feet on earth would one day have hands reaching among the stars."

When darkness fell over the earth in these last few years, he turned to pessimism. "There is no reason whatever to believe that the order of nature has any greater bias in favor of man than it had in favor of the ichthyosaur. In spite of all my disposition to a brave looking optimism, I perceive that now the universe is bored with him, is turning a hard face to him, and I see him being carried less and less intelligently, and more and more rapidly . . . along the stream of fate to degradation, suffering, and death."

Now hear St. Paul, who already had been persecuted, and who knew that the tyrant who held the sword would one day draw it across his neck:

"We are reviled: and we bless. We are persecuted: and we suffer it.

"We are blasphemed: and we entreat. We are made as the refuse of this world".

(1Corinthians 4:12-13)

"Who then shall separate us from the love of Christ? Shall tribulation? Or distress? Or famine? Or nakedness? Or danger? Or persecution? Or the sword?

“For I am sure that neither death, nor life, nor Angels, nor principalities, nor powers, nor things present, nor things to come, nor might.

“Nor height, nor depth, nor any other creature, shall be able to separate us from the love of God which is in Christ Jesus our Lord”

(Romans 8:35,38-39)

Take another comparison in time of trouble. Hear Bertrand Russell, a typical modern without faith in God. What is his hope for man?

“Man's origin, his growth, his hopes, fears, his loves, and beliefs, are but the outcome of accidental collocation of atoms. That no fire, no heroism, no intensity of thought and feeling, can preserve the individual beyond the grave; that all the labor of the ages, all devotion, all the inspiration, all the noonday brightness of human genius are destined to extinction, and that the whole temple of Man's achievement must be buried beneath the debris of a universe in ruins. Only on the firm foundation of unyielding despair can the soul's habitation be safely built.”

Now turn to St. Augustine who lived in a world of despair when the Roman Empire that had survived for centuries fell, even as Satan fell from heaven, to the barbarians from the North.

“God, Who is not the Author of evil, but Who allowest it to exist in order to prevent greater evil.

“God Who art loved, knowingly or unknowingly, by everything that is capable of loving.

"God, in Whom all things are, yet Who receivest from the ignominy of creatures, no ignominy, from their malice, no malice, from their errors, no errors.

"God, from Whom to turn is to fall, towards Whom to turn, is to rise again, in Whom to dwell, is to find firm support; from Whom to depart is to die, to return to Whom, is to be restored to life, to dwell in Whom, is to live.

"God, Whom to forsake is the same as to perish, Whom to search for is the same as to love, Whom to see is the same as to possess.

"God, towards Whom faith, urges, hope raises us, charity unites us. God, through Whom we triumph over our enemy.

"Thee I invoke.

"To Thee, I address my prayers."

You see the difference! Now choose! Will you slip down into abysmal despair, or will you, like Christ in a blackness at high noon, and like Mary ere her Tree of Life had seen the earth, trust in God, His Mercy and His Victory?

If you are unhappy, or sad, or despondent, it is basically for only one reason: you have refused to respond to Love's plea: "Come to me, all you that labor and are burdened, and I will refresh you. Take up my yoke upon you and learn of me, because I am meek, and humble of heart: and you shall find rest to your souls" *(Matthew 11:28-29)*. Everywhere else but in Him, the liberation promised is either armed or forced, and that can mean slavery. Only *nailed* love is free. Unnailed and uncrucified love can compel. Hands pinioned to a wooden beam cannot compel, nor can a lifted Host and an elevated Chalice constrain, but they can beckon and solicit.

That kind of love gives you these three suggestions for living in troubled times:

1) Never forget that there are only two philosophies to rule your life: the one of the Cross, which starts with the fast and ends with the feast. The other of Satan, which starts with the feast and ends with the headache. Unless there is the Cross, there will never be the empty tomb; unless there is faith in darkness, there will never be vision in light; unless there is a Good Friday, there will never be an Easter Sunday. In the beautiful assurance of our Lord: "Amen, amen, I say to you, that you shall lament and weep, but the world shall rejoice: and you shall be made sorrowful, but your sorrow shall be turned into joy " *(John 16:20)*.

2) When bereavement comes, and when the "slings and arrows of outrageous fortune" strike, when like Simon of Cyrene a cross is laid on your reluctant shoulders, take that Cross to daily Mass and say to our Lord at the moment of consecration: "As Thou my Saviour in love for me dost say: 'This is My Body! This is My Blood!' so I say to Thee: 'This is my body! Take it. This is my blood! Take it. They are yours. I care not if the accidents or species of my life remain, with my daily work, my routine duties. But all that I am substantially, take, consecrate, ennoble, spiritualize; turn my cross into a Crucifix, so that I am no longer mine, but Thine, O Love Divine!'"

3) Think not of Almighty God as a kind of absentee landlord with whom you hardly dare to be familiar, or to whom you go to fix your leaks,

or to get yourself out of a mess. Think neither of God as an insurance agent, who can protect you against loss by fire. Approach Him not timidly as a stenographer might approach the boss for a raise, fearful, half believing that you will never receive what you seek. Do not fear Him with a servile fear, for God is more patient with you than you are with yourself. Would you, for example, be as patient with the wicked world today as He is? Would you even be as patient with anyone else who had the same faults as you? Rather, approach Him in full confidence and even with the boldness of a loving child who has a right to ask a Father for favors.

Though He may not grant all your wants, be sure that, in a certain sense, there is no unanswered prayer. A child asks his father for something that may not be good for him, e.g., a gun. The father, while refusing, will pick up the child in his arms to console him, giving the response of love, even in the denial of a request. As the child forgets in that embrace that he ever asked a favor, so in praying, you forget what you wanted by receiving what you needed — a return of love. Do not forget either that there are not two kinds of answers to prayer, but three: One is "Yes." Another is "No." The third is "Wait."

You will find that, as you pray, the nature of your requests will change. You will ask less and less things for yourself and more and more for His love. Is it not true in human relationships that the more you love someone, the more you seek to give, and the less you desire to receive? The deepest love never says: "Give me," but it does say: "Make me." You probably think that if Our Lord came into your room some night as you are praying, you would ask Him favors, or present your difficulties, or say: "When will the war end?" or "Should I buy General Motors stock? " or "Give me a million."

No! You would throw yourself on your knees and kiss the hem of His garment. And the moment He laid His hands on your head, you would feel such a peace and trust and confidence — even in darkness — that you would not even remember you had questions to ask, or favors to beg. You would consider them a kind of desecration. You would want only to look into His face, and you would be in a world which only lovers know. That would be the only Heaven you wanted! (8)

The Seven Words of Jesus and Mary, 1945

THE SUFFERING OF THE INNOCENT

"Woman, behold thy son!

(Son) Behold thy mother!"

Why do the innocent suffer? We do not mean the innocent who have suffering involuntarily thrust upon them, but rather those good souls who go out in search of suffering and are impatient until they find a cross. In other words, why should there be Carmelites, Poor Clares, Trappists, Little Sisters of the Poor, and dozens of penitential orders of the Church, who do nothing but sacrifice and suffer for the sins of men?

Certainly not because suffering is necessarily connected with personal sin. Our Lord told us that much, when to those who asked concerning a blind boy, "Who hath sinned, this man, or his parents . . .?" Our Lord answered "Neither."

If we are to find the answer we must go not merely to the suffering of innocent people, but to the suffering of Innocence itself. In this *Third Word* our attention is riveted upon the two most sinless creatures who ever trod our sinful earth: Jesus and Mary.

Jesus Himself was sinless by nature, for He is the all-holy Son of God. Mary was sinless by grace, for she is "our tainted nature's solitary boast." And yet both suffer in the extreme. Why did He suffer Who had the power of God to escape the Cross? Why did she suffer who could have dispensed herself because of her virtue, or could have been excused by her Divine Son?

Love is the key to the mystery. Love by its very nature is not selfish, but generous. It seeks not its own, but the good of others. The measure of love is not the pleasure it gives -- that is the way the world judges it -- but the joy and peace it can purchase for others.

It counts not the wine it drinks, but the wine it serves. Love is not a circle circumscribed by self; it is a cross with arms embracing all humanity. It thinks not of having, but of being had, not of possessing but of being possessed, not of owning but of being owned.

Love then by its nature is social. Its greatest happiness is to gird its loins and serve at the banquet of life. Its greatest unhappiness is to be denied the joy of sacrifice for others. *That is why in the face of pain, love seeks to unburden the sufferer and take his pain, and that is why in the face of sin, love seeks to atone for the injustice of him who sinned.*

Because mothers love, do they not want to take the pain of their children's wounds? Because fathers love, do they not take over the debts of wayward sons to expiate their foolishness?

What does all this mean but the "otherness" of love? In fact love is so social it would reject emancipation from pain, if the emancipation were for itself alone. Love refuses to accept individual salvation; it never bends over man, as the healthy over the sick, but enters into him to take his very sickness.

It refuses to have its eyes clear, when other eyes are bedewed with tears; it cannot be happy unless everyone is happy, or unless justice is served; it shrinks from isolation and aloofness from the burdens and hungers of others. It spurns insulation from the shock of the world's sorrow, but insinuates itself into them, as if the sorrow were its very own.

This is not difficult to understand. Would you want to be the only person in all the world who had eyes to see? Would you want to be the only one who could walk in a universe of the lame? Would you, if you loved your family, stand on the dock and watch them all drown before your very eyes?

And if not, why not? Very simply, because you love them, because you feel so much one with them that their heartaches are your own heartbreaks.

Now apply this to Our Lord and His Blessed Mother. Here is love at its peak and innocence at its best.

Can they be indifferent to that which is a greater evil than pain, namely sin? Can they watch humanity carry a cross to the Golgotha of death, while they themselves refuse to share its weight? Can they be indifferent to the outcome of love if they themselves *are* Love? If love means identification and sympathy with the one loved, then why should not God so love the world as to send His only begotten Son into it to redeem the world? And if that Divine Son loved the world enough to die for it, why should not the Mother of Love Incarnate share that redemption? If human love identifies itself with the pain of the one loved, why should not Divine Love suffer when it comes in contact with sin in man? If mothers suffer in their children, if a husband grieves in the sorrow of his wife, and if friends feel the agony of their beloved's cross, why should not Jesus and Mary suffer in the humanity they love?

If you would die for your family of which you are the head, why should not He die for humanity of which He is the Head? And if the deeper the love the more poignant the pain, why should not the Crucifixion be born of that Love?

If a sensitive nerve is touched it registers pain in the brain; and since Our Lord is the Head of suffering humanity, He felt every sin of every man as His own. That is why the Cross was inevitable.

He could not love us perfectly unless He died for us. And His Mother could not love Him perfectly, unless she shared that death. That is why His life was given for us, and her heart broken for us; and that, too, is why He is Redeemer and she is Redemptrix -- because they love.

In order more completely to reveal that a Cross was made up of the juncture of Love and sin, Our Lord spoke His *Third Word* to His Mother: "Woman, behold thy son"! He did not call her 'Mother' but 'Woman'; except when addressing John the next moment He added: "[Son] Behold thy Mother."

The term 'Woman' indicated a wider relationship to all humanity than 'Mother.' It meant that she was to be not only His Mother, but that she was also to be the Mother of all men, as He was the Saviour of all men. She was now to have many children -- not according to the flesh, but according to the spirit. Jesus was her first-born of the flesh in joy; John was her second-born of the spirit in sorrow; and we her millionth and millionth born.

If she loved Him Who died for all men, then she must love those for whom He died. That was His clear, unmistakable meaning. The love of neighbor is inseparable from the love of God. His love had no limits; He died for every man. Her love then must have no limits.

It must not be merely unselfish; it must even be social. She must be the Mother of every man. An earthly mother loves her own children most, but Jesus is now telling her that even John is her son, too, and John was the symbol of all of us.

The Father did not spare His Son, nor did the Son spare His Mother, for love knows no bounds. Jesus had a sense of responsibility for every soul in the world; Mary, too, inspired by His love, had a corresponding sense of responsibility. If He would be the Redeemer of the wayward children, she must be their Mother.

Now does that throw any light on the problem? Why do innocent, pure, good souls leave the world and its pleasures, feast on fasts, embrace the cross, and pray their hearts out? The answer is, *because they love.* "Greater love than this no man hath, that a man lay down his life for his friends."

They love the world so much that they want to save it, and they know there is no other way to save it, than to die for it. Many of us so love the world that we live *in* it and are *of* it, but in the end do nothing *for* it. Wrong indeed are they who say these innocent victims hate the world.

As soon as the world hears of a beautiful young woman or an upright young man entering the religious life, it asks: "Why did they leave the world?" They left the world, not because they hated the world, but because they loved it. They love the world with its human souls so much, that they want to do all they can for it; and they can do nothing better for it than to pray that souls may one day find their way back to God.

Our Lord did not hate the world; it hated Him. But He loved it. Neither do they hate the world; they are in love with it and everyone in it. They so much love the sinners in it, that they expiate for their sins; they so much love the Communists in it, that they bless them as they send them to their God; they so much love the atheists in it, that they are willing to surrender the joy of the divine presence that the atheist may feel less afraid in the dark.

They are so much lovers of the world that they may be said to be organic with it. They know that things and souls are so much interrelated that the good which one does has repercussion on the millions, just as ten just men could have saved Sodom and Gomorrah. If a stone is thrown into the sea, it causes a ripple which widens in ever greater circles until it affects even the most distant shore; a rattle dropped from a baby's crib affects even the most distant star; a finger is burnt and the whole body feels the pain.

The cosmos then is organic; but so also is humanity. We are all called to be members of a great family.

God is Our Father, Who sent His Son into the world to be Our Brother, and He on the Cross asked Mary to be Our Mother. Now if in the human body it is possible to graft skin from one member to another, why is it not possible also to graft prayer?

If it is possible to transfuse blood, why is it not possible also to transfuse sacrifice? Why cannot the innocent atone for the sinful?

Why cannot the real lovers of souls, who refuse to be emancipated from sorrow, do for the world what Jesus did on the cross and Mary did beneath it? The answer to this question has filled the cloisters.

No one on earth can measure the good these divine lovers are doing for the world. How often have they stayed the wrath of a righteous God! How many sinners have they brought to the confessional! How many deathbed conversions have they effected! How many persecutions have they averted!

We do not know, and they do not want to know, so long as love wins over hate. But let us not be foolish and ask: What good do they do for the world? We might as well ask: What good did the Cross do?

After all, only the innocent can understand what sin is. No one until the time of Our Lord ever thought of giving his life to save sinners, simply because no one was sinless enough to know its horrors.

We who have familiarized ourselves with it, become used to it, as a leprous patient after many years of suffering cannot wholly appreciate the evil of leprosy.

Sin has lost its horror; we never think of correlating it to the cross: we never advert to its repercussions on humanity.

"Vice is a monster of so frightful mien,

As to be hated, needs but to be seen;

Yet seen too oft, familiar with her face,

We first endure, then pity, then embrace."

(Alexander Pope)

The best way to know sin is by not sinning. But Jesus and Mary were wholly innocent -- He by nature, she by grace; therefore they could understand and know the evil of sin.

Having never compromised with it, there were now no compromises to be made. It was something so awful that to avoid it or to atone for it, they shrink not even from a death on the cross.

But by a peculiar paradox, though innocence hates sin, because it alone knows its gravity, it nevertheless loves the sinner. Jesus loved Peter who fell three times, and Mary chose as her companion at the foot of the cross, a converted prostitute.

What must the scandal mongers have said of that friendship as they watched Mary and Magdalen ascend and descend the hill of Calvary! But Mary braved it all, in order that in a future generation you and I might have hope in her as the "Refuge of sinners." Let there be no fear that she cannot understand our sinful misery because she is Immaculate, for if she had Magdalen as a companion then, why can she not have us now?

Dear Mother Immaculate, but seldom in history have the innocent suffered as they do today. Countless Marys and Johns stand beneath the cross guilty of no other crime than that they love the Man on the Cross. If there be no remission of sins without the shedding of blood, then let these innocent victims of hate in Russia, in Spain, and in Mexico, be the redemption of those who hate. We ask not that the hateful perish; we only ask that the sufferings of the just be the salvation of the wicked.

Thou didst suffer innocently because thou didst love us in union with thy Divine Son. Thus were we taught, that only those who cease to love ever flee from the Cross. The innocents who are slaughtered today are not the babes of Bethlehem; they are the grown-up children of Bethlehem's God -- men and women who save the Church today as Bethlehem's babes once saved Jesus.

Be thou their consolation, their joy, their Mother, O Innocent Woman who binds the sons of men to the Son of God in the unity of the Father and the Holy Ghost, world without end. Amen. (9)

The Rainbow of Sorrow, 1938

RELIGION IS A QUEST

The Fifth Word from The Cross

"I Thirst." (John 19:28)

The Blessed Virgin Mary's Response

And seeing him, they wondered. And his mother said to him: Son, why hast thou done so to us? Behold thy father and I have sought thee sorrowing. (Luke 2:48)

EVERY HUMAN HEART in the world without exception is on the quest of God. Not everyone may be conscious of it; but they are conscious of their desire for happiness which some in ignorance, perversity, or weakness identify with the tinsel and baubles of earth. It is as natural for the soul to want God as for the body to want food or drink. It was natural for the prodigal son to be hungry; it was unnatural to live on husks. It is natural to want God; it is unnatural to satisfy that want with false gods.

On the other hand, not only is the soul on the quest of God, but God is on the quest of the soul, inviting everyone to His Banquet of Love. But since love is free, His invitation is rejected in the Gospel language either because they have just married, or because they have bought a farm, or because they must try a yoke of oxen.

This double quest of the Creator for the creature and the creature for the Creator is revealed in the Fifth Word of our Lord from the Cross, and the Fifth Word of our Lady, pronounced when her Son was only twelve years of age.

One day Our Blessed Lord said to the multitude: "If any man thirst, let him come to me and drink" *(John 7:37)*. But on the Cross, He, from whose fingertips toppled planets and worlds, He Who filled the valleys with the song of a thousand fountains now cries, not to God, but to man: "I thirst" *(John 19:28)*. The physical pain of being nailed to a cross, lingering for hours without food or drink beneath an Oriental sun, the parched dryness that came from loss of blood, now expresses itself not in peevish impatience but in a simple declaration of thirst.

There is nothing in the whole story of the Crucifixion which makes Our Lord seem so human as this one Word. And yet that thirst could not have been only physical, for the Gospel tells us that He said it in order that the Scriptures might be fulfilled. It, therefore, was spiritual as well as physical. God was on the quest of souls, trusting that one of the trivial ministrations of life, the offering of a cup in His name, might bring the offering within the sweet radiance of His Grace. The Shepherd was still out after the sheep, at the moment when He was giving His Life for the flock!

Mary standing in the shadow of her Son's hard deathbed heard His Word and knew that it was more than a plea for relief. She remembered so well the Psalm from which it was taken. Hearing it, she was reminded of the time she thirsted, too. It was just when her little Son reached the legal age of twelve. During the Feast of the unleavened bread, instituted in remembrance of the Exodus from Egypt, Mary and Joseph joined the pilgrimage to the Holy City. After seven days, according to custom, the multitude departed in the afternoon, the men leaving by one gate, the women by another, to reunite at the halting-place of the first night. Joseph and Mary left, each thinking the Child was with the other, only to discover at nightfall that He was not with either.

If the trumpets of doom had sounded, their hearts would have been less heavy. For three days they flushed the hills and the caravans, and on the third day, they found Him. We know not where He was during those three days. We can only guess. Perhaps He was visiting Gethsemani where His Blood, twenty-one years later would crimson the olive roots; perhaps He stood on Calvary's hill and saw this sad hour. In any case, on the third day, they found Him in the temple, teaching the doctors of the law. Mary said: "Son, why hast thou done so to us? Behold thy father, and I have sought thee sorrowing" (*Luke 2:48*). In a land where women were reticent, where men were always masters, it was not Joseph who spoke. It was Mary. Mary was the mother; Joseph was the foster-father.

When Abraham drew near to God, a "great and darksome horror seized upon him" *(Genesis 15:12)*, and when the Lord appeared, "Abraham fell flat on his face" *(Genesis 17:3)*. When Jacob saw the Lord, he trembled saying: "How terrible is this place" *(Genesis 28:17)*. When Moses came in the presence of God, "Moses hid his face" *(Exodus 3:6)*. And yet here, a woman addresses Him Who is the Author of Life, through whom all things were made and without Whom nothing is made, as "*Son*." She called Him that by right and not by privilege. That one word shows the intimate relationship between the two, and it was probably her usual way of addressing Him in Nazareth.

Here was a creature on the quest of God. As our Blessed Lord's thirst on the Cross revealed the Creator in search of man, Mary's words revealed its complementary truth that the creature is in search of God.

If each is seeking for the other, why do they not find? God does not always find man because man is free, and like Adam man can hide from God. Like a child who hides from his mother when he does something wrong so does man turn from God when he sins. God then always seems "so far away;" but the truth is, it is man who is "far away." Sin creates a distance. Respecting human freedom, God calls, but He does not force. "I thirst" is the language of liberty.

God is closer to us than we suspect, as Paul told the Athenians. He may be somewhat disguised and appear like a gardener as He did to Mary Magdalen, or like a chance acquaintance on a roadway, as He did to the disciples of Emmaus. What must have been the chagrin, therefore, of the inn-keepers of Bethlehem when they discovered that they had refused hospitality to the Mother of Our Lord! If they ever met Our Blessed Mother, later on, they probably chided her saying: "Why did you not tell us that you were the Mother of Jesus?" If any of the bystanders at the Crucifixion within the next forty days saw the Risen and Glorified Saviour, how they must have mourned in their hearts, saying: "If I had only known, it was You Who asked for a drink."

Why is it that in religion we want a proof and a manifestation so strong that it will overwhelm our reason and destroy our freedom? That God will never grant! On man's side, the regret will continue even until Judgment! When Christ shall say: "I was thirsty, and you gave me not to drink" *(Matthew 25:42)*.

"The angels keep their ancient places;

Turn but a stone, and start a wing!

'Tis ye, 'tis your estranged faces,

That miss the many-splendored thing."

From the Fifth Word of Jesus and Mary, there emerges the lesson that the apostolate of religion should start with the assumption that everyone wants God. Bigots? Do they want Our Lord and His Church? Certainly, they think more about the Church than some who belong to it. Be not too hard on them.

They do not really hate the Church. They hate only what they mistakenly believe to be the Church. If I had heard the same lies about the Church that they have heard, and if I had been taught the same historical perversions as they, with my own peculiar character and temperament, I would hate the Church ten times more than they do. At least they have some zeal and some fire. It may be misdirected, but with God's grace, it can be channeled into love as well as hate.

These souls who peddle anti-religion tracts or anti-Catholic publications are to be regarded in exactly the same light as St. Paul before his conversion. And as he preached and lectured against the Church, after assisting at the killing of the most brilliant of the early Churchmen, St. Stephen, there were many believers who despaired. Prayers were multiplied to God: "Send someone to refute Paul." And God heard their prayers God sent Paul to answer Paul. A bigot made the best Apostle.

In my radio audience a few years ago was a young woman who used to sit before the radio and ridicule and scoff and wisecrack at every word. She is now enjoying the fullness of Faith and the Sacraments. In another town was a man who used to make records of these broadcasts, then take them to a nearby convent, and play them for the sisters, who had no radio. But he mitigated this act of kindness by making a running commentary of ridicule while the record played. He recently built the new Sisters' school in that city. Everyone is on the quest of God, and if the soul gives God a chance, God will win.

God is thirsting too, for those who have lost the Faith. The position of the fallen-away Catholic is rather unique. The seriousness of his fall is to be measured by the heights from which he fell. His reaction to the Church is either hate or argument. In both cases, he bears witness to the Divinity of the Church. The hate is his vain attempt to despise. Since his conscience, which was informed by the Spirit in the Church, will not let him alone, he will not let the Church alone.

But the general truth still holds true: assume that he is on the quest of the Divine. Otherwise he would not think so much about it. Hence never, never, never argue with a fallen away Catholic. He may tell you, for example, that he left because he could not believe in Confession. Do not believe it. He left because he refused in his pride to confess his sins. He wants to argue to salve his conscience, but he needs absolution to heal it. Like the woman at the well, who had five husbands, he wants to keep religion in the realm of the speculative. What he needs is to have it brought down in the realm of the moral, as our Blessed Lord did for that woman. His difficulty is not with the Creed: it is with the commandments. Having tasted the best, he is miserable without it.

We do not help him by telling him why the road he took was wrong. He knows it. He even knows the right road. We can help him best, like the father of the prodigal, by going out on the road to meet him and make the return journey easy, for every prodigal wants to get back home.

Sinners too, want God. That is to say, conscious sinners. One need hardly ever tell such a sinner how wicked he is. He knows it a thousand times better than you. His conscience has pointed an accusing finger at him in his sleep; his fears have emblazoned his sins on his mind; his neurosis, anxieties, and unhappiness have been like trumpets of his inner death.

This consciousness of sin is not yet conversion, for up to this point a soul may be repenting like Judas, only to itself. One can be mad at oneself for playing the fool, or be ashamed at one's misdeeds, or be sad at being discovered, but there is no true repentance without a turning to God. The consciousness of sin creates the vacuum; grace alone can fill it.

You say: "I am a sinner. I will not be heard." If God will not hear a sinner, why did he praise the publican in the rear of the Temple, who struck his breast saying: "O God, be merciful to me a sinner" *(Luke 18:13)* There were two sinners on Calvary on either side of our Lord. One was saved because he asked to be saved. Did not our Divine Saviour say: "Come to me, all you that labor and are burdened" *(Matthew 11:28)* — and who is more heavily burdened than a sinner? Unlike all other religions, Christianity starts with the sinner. In a certain sense, it begins with human hopelessness. You have to be good to enter most other religions; you become a Christian on the assumption that you are not good.

God will find you if your will does not refuse to be found. Hence, avoid those selfish and petty acts which may deaden and stunt you in the one great moment, when surrender to the Divine Will can bring peace. In that case, we become like the cobbler of Charles Dickens. For years he had been a prisoner in the Bastille, where he cobbled shoes. He became so enamored of the walls, the darkness, and the task's monotony that when he was liberated, he built a cell at the center of his English home. On days when skies were clear, and birds were singing, the taps of the cobbler in the dark could still be heard. So men, by habitual residence in imprisoning moods, render themselves incapable of living in wider horizons, the great hopes, and faith of religion.

Stunt not your spiritual life by looking for faults. You do not say Shakespeare cannot write because you heard a poor actor butcher the soliloquy of Hamlet; you do not reject the beauty of music because you hear an occasional moaner or groaner on the radio; you do not disbelieve in medicine because your doctor has a cold.

Give God a chance. The prolongation of his Incarnate Life in the Church is an offer, not a demand. It is a gift, not a bargain. You can never deserve it, but you can receive it. God is on the quest of your soul. Whether you will know peace depends on your own will. "If any man will do the will of him, he shall know of the doctrine, whether it be of God, or whether I speak of myself" *(John 7:17).* (10)

The Seven Words of Jesus and Mary, 1945

LUST

“Woman, behold thy son . . . behold thy mother.”

Lust is an inordinate love of the pleasures of the flesh. The important word here is *inordinate* for it was Almighty God Himself who associated pleasure with the flesh. He attached pleasure to eating in order that we might not be remiss in nourishing and preserving our individual lives; He associated pleasure with the marital act in order that husband and wife might not be remiss in their social obligations to propagate mankind and raise children for the Kingdom of God.

The pleasure becomes sinful at that point where, instead of using it as means, we begin to use it as an end. To eat for the sake of eating is a sin, because eating is a means to an end, which is health. Lust, in like manner, is selfishness or perverted love.

It looks not so much to the good of the other, as to the pleasure of self. It breaks the glass that holds the wine; it breaks the lute to snare the music. It subordinates the other to self for the sake of pleasure. Denying the quality of "otherness," it seeks to make the other person care for us, but not to make us care for the other person.

We are living today in what might properly be called an era of carnality. As the appeal to the spiritual relaxes, the demands of the flesh increase. Living less for God, human nature begins to live only for self, for "no man can serve two masters: For either he will hate the one, and love the other: or he will sustain the one, and despise the other."

Peculiar to this era of carnality is the tendency to equate the perpetuity of marriage with the fleshly pleasure, so that when the pleasure ends the bond is presumed to be automatically dissolved. In America, for example, there is more than one divorce for every four marriages -- an indication of how much we have ceased to be a Christian nation and how much we have forgotten the words of Our Lord: "What therefore God hath joined together, let no man put asunder."

The regrettable aspect of it all is that with this increased sin there is a decreased sense of sin. Souls sin more, but think less about it. Like sick who are so moribund that they have no desire to be better, sinners become so calloused they have no yearning for redemption. Having lost their eyes, they no longer want to see; the only pleasure left them in the end is to mock and sneer at those who do.

It is never the pure who say that chastity is impossible, but only the impure. We judge others by ourselves, and attribute to others the vices from which we ourselves refuse to abstain.

Some reparation had to be made for the sin of lust which in Old Testament times became so hideous to God that He would have withheld the destruction of the cities of Sodom and Gomorrah could but ten just men have been found within their gates.

Our Lord began making reparation for it at the first moment of the Incarnation for He chose to be born of a virgin. Why did He choose to transcend the laws of nature? The answer is very simple. Original Sin has been propagated to every human being from Adam to this very hour, with the exception of Our Lady. The prolongation of this taint in human nature takes place through the carnal act, of which man is the active principle, for man was the head of the human race. Every time there is generation of one human being by another, through the union of man and woman, there is the propagation of original sin.

The problem confronting the Second Person of the Blessed Trinity in becoming man was: how become man without at the same time becoming sinful man, that is, man-infected by the sin to which all flesh is heir? How to become man without inheriting original sin? He had to be a true man in order to suffer for man, but He could not be a sinful man if He were to redeem man from sin. How could He be both man and yet sinless?

He could be man by being born of a woman; He could be sinless man, without original sin, by dispensing with man as the active principle of generation -- in other words, by being born of a virgin. Thus it was that when the Angel Gabriel appeared to Mary and told her that she was to conceive the Messias whose name would be called Jesus, she answered: "How can this be done, because I know not man?" She had made the vow of virginity and she intended to keep it.

The Angel answered that the conception of the Son of Man would take place without man, through the power of the Holy Ghost who would overshadow her. Being assured of her continued virginity, she accepted the motherhood of God Incarnate. "Be it done unto me, according to thy word."

So it was that reparation for sins of the flesh began the first moment of the Incarnation through the Virgin Birth. That same love He manifested for virginity in the beginning, He re-echoed in the first sermon of His public life: "Blessed are the clean of heart: for they shall see God."

Later on, to the Scribes and Pharisees who sought to malign His good name, He challenged them to find anything impure in His life: "Which of you shall convince me of sin?"

The final atonement and reparation is made on Calvary where, in reparation for all the impure desires and thoughts of men, Our Lord is crowned with thorns; where, in reparation for all the sins of shame, He is stripped of His garments; where, in reparation for all the lusts of the flesh, He is almost dispossessed of His flesh, for according to Sacred Scripture, the very bones of His Body could be numbered.

We are so used to looking upon artistic crucifixes of ivory and the beautiful images in our prayer books, that we think of Our Blessed Lord as being whole on the Cross. The fact is that He made such reparation for sins of the flesh that His Body was torn, His Blood poured forth, and Scripture refers to Him on the Cross as a leper, as one struck by God and afflicted, so that "there is no beauty in Him, nor comeliness . . . that we should be desirous of Him."

Our Lord chose to go even further in reparation for the sins of lust by dispossessing Himself of the two most legitimate claims of the flesh. If there was ever a pure and legitimate claim in the realm of the flesh, it is the claim to the love of one's own Mother. If there is any honest title to affection in the universe of the flesh, it is the bonds of love that attach one to a fellow man. But the flesh was so misused by man and so perverted that Our Divine Saviour renounced even these legitimate bonds of the flesh in order to atone for the illegitimate.

He became totally un-fleshed, in order to atone for the abuse of the flesh, by giving away His Mother and His best friend. So, to His own

Mother He looks and bids farewell: "Woman, behold thy son"; and to His best friend He looks and bids farewell again: "Behold thy mother."

How different from the world! A mother will deprive her son of an advanced education in a foreign land, saying: "I cannot give up my son"; or a wife will deprive her husband of good material advancement through a short absence, saying: "I cannot give up my husband." These are not the cries of noble love but of attachment. Our Lord did not say: "I cannot give up My Mother." He gave her up. He loved her enough to give her away for her life's plan and destiny, namely, to be *our* Mother.

Here was a love that was strong enough to forget itself, in order that others might never want for love. He made the sacrifice of His Mother that we might have her; He wounded Himself like the pelican, that we might be nourished by her motherhood. Mary accepted the poor exchange to carry out her Son's redemptive work. And at that moment when Jesus surrendered even the legitimate claims of the flesh and gave us His Mother, Mary, and His best friend, John -- selfishness died its death.

Two lessons are to be learned from this Third Word from the Cross:

1 -- The only real escape from the demands of the flesh is to find something more than the flesh to love; and 2 -- Mary is the refuge of sinners.

If we could ever find anything we loved more than the flesh, the demands of the flesh would be less imperative. This is the "escape" a mother offers her boy when she says: "Don't do anything of which your mother would ever be ashamed." If there is that higher love of his mother, the boy will always have a consecrated sense of affection, something for which he will be willing to make sacrifices.

When a mother makes such an appeal to her son she is merely re-echoing the lesson of the Saviour, who, in giving His Mother to us as our Mother, equivalently said: "My children, never do anything of which your Mother would be ashamed." Let a soul but love that Mother and He will love her Divine Son Jesus, Who, in order to make satisfaction for the unlawful pleasure of the flesh, surrendered to us His last and lawful attachment -- His Mother.

The psychology of this enthusiasm for a higher love of Jesus and Mary as an escape from the unlawful attachments of the flesh is this: by it we avoid undue concentration on lower loves and their explosions. Think about your mouth for five minutes, and you will have an undue concentration of saliva. Think about your heart for five minutes and you will believe you have heart trouble, though the chances are nine out of ten that you have not. Stand on a stage and think about your hands and they will begin to feel as big as hams.

The balance and equilibrium of the whole system is disturbed when an organ is isolated from its function in the whole organism, or divorced from its higher purpose. Those people who are always talking, reading, and thinking about sex are like singers who think more about their larynx than about singing. They make that which is subordinate to a higher purpose so all important that the harmony of life is upset.

But suppose that, instead of concentrating on an organ, one fitted that organ into a pattern of living -- then all the uneasiness would end. The skilled orator never feels his hands are awkward because, being enthused about his speech, he makes his hands subordinate to their higher purpose.

Our Lord practically said the same thing: "Be not solicitous . . . what you shall eat." So it is with the flesh. Cultivate a higher love, a purpose of living, a goal of existence, a desire to correspond to all that God wants us to be, and the lower passion will be absorbed by it.

The Church applies this psychology to the vow of chastity. The Church asks her priests and nuns to surrender even the lawful pleasures of the flesh, not because she does not want them to love, but because she wants them to love better. She knows that their love for souls will be greater as their love for the flesh is less, just as Our Lord died on the Cross for men because He loved His Own life less.

Nor must it be thought that the vow of chastity is a burden. Thompson has called it a "passionless passion, a wild tranquility." And so it is. A new passion is born with the vow of chastity, the passion for the love of God. It is the consolation of that higher love which makes the surrender of the lower love so easy. And only when that higher love is lost does the vow begin to be a burden, just as honesty becomes a burden only to those who have lost the sense of others' rights.

The reason there is a degeneration in the moral order and a decay of decency is because men and women have lost the higher love. Ignoring Christ their Saviour, who loved them unto the death on Calvary, and Mary who loved them unto becoming Queen of Martyrs beneath that Cross, they have nothing for which to make the sacrifice.

The only way love can be shown in this world is by sacrifice, namely, the surrender of one thing for another. Love is essentially bound up with choice, and choice is a negation, and negation is a sacrifice. When a young man sets his heart upon a maid and asks her to marry him, he is not only saying "I choose you"; he is also saying "I do not choose, I reject, all others. I give them all up for you." Apply this to the problem of lust.

Take away all love above the flesh, take away God, the crucifix, the Sorrowful Mother, salvation, eternal happiness -- and what possibility is there for choice, what is to be gained by denying the imperious and revolutionary demands of the flesh? But grant the Divine, and the flesh's greatest joy is to throw itself on the altar of the one loved where it counts its sorrow a cheap price for the blissful joy of giving.

Then its greatest despair is not to be needed; it could almost find it in its heart to inflict a wound that it might bind and heal. Such is the attitude of the pure: they have integrated their flesh with the Divine; they have sublimated its cravings with the Cross; having a higher love, they now make the surrender of the lower, that their Mother may never be put to shame.

Mary is the refuge of sinners. She who is the Virgin Most Pure is also the Refuge of Sinners. She knows what sin is, not by the experience of its falls, not by tasting its bitter regrets, but by seeing what it did to her Divine Son.

She looked upon His torn and bleeding flesh hanging from Him like rays of a purple sunset -- and she came to know how much flesh sinned by seeing what His flesh suffered. What better way in all the world was there to measure the heinousness of sin than by seeing when left alone with Him for three hours, what it could do to Innocence and Purity.

She is the Refuge of Sinners not only because she knows sin through Calvary, but also because she chose, during the most terrifying hours of her life, a converted sinner as her companion. The measure of our appreciation of friends is our desire to have them about us in the moment of our greatest need.

Mary heard Jesus say, "The harlots and publicans will enter the Kingdom of Heaven before the Scribes and Pharisees." So she chose the absolved harlot, Magdalen, as her companion at the Cross. What the scandalmongers of that day must have said when they saw Our Blessed Mother in the company of a woman who everyone knew was the kind who sold her body without giving away her soul.

Magdalen knew that day why Mary is the Refuge of Sinners, and certainly our day, too, can learn that if she had Magdalen as a companion then, she is willing to have us as companions now.

Mary's purity is not a holier-than-thou purity, a stand-offish holiness that gathers up its robes lest they be stained by the sinful; nor is it a despising purity which looks down upon the impure. Rather, it is a radiating purity that is no more spoiled by solicitude for the fallen than a ray of sunshine is sullied by a dirty window pane through which it pours.

There is no reason for the fallen to be discouraged. Hope is the message of Golgotha. Find a higher love than the flesh, a love pure, understanding, redeeming, and the struggle will be easy. That higher love is on the Cross and beneath it.

We almost seem to forget that there is a Cross at all. He begins to look more like a red rose and she begins to look like the stem. That stem reaches down from Calvary into all our wounded hearts of earth, sucking up our prayers and petitions and conveying them to Him. That is why roses have thorns in this life -- to keep away every disturbing influence that might destroy our union with Jesus and Mary.

ACKNOWLEDGEMENT

If Christ should come on earth some summer day
And walk unknown upon our busy street
I wonder how 'twould be if we should meet,
And being God – if He would act that way.

Perhaps the kindest thing that He would do
Would be just to forget I failed to pray
And clasp my hand, forgivingly, and say,
"My child, I've heard My Mother speak of you."

(Mrs. Frederick V. Murphy) (11)

Victory Over Vice, 1939

THE HOUR

The Sixth Word from the Cross

"It Is Finished." (John 19:30)

The Blessed Virgin Mary's Response

"They have no wine." (John 2:3)

THE MOST CURRENT philosophy of life today is self-expressionism: "Let yourself go;" "Do whatever you please." Any suggestion of restraining errant impulses is called a masochistic survival of the dark ages. The truth is that the only really self-expressive people in the world are in the insane asylum. They have absolutely no inhibitions, no conventions, and no codes. They are as self-expressive as hell, i.e., in complete disorder.

Self-expressive lives in this sense are self-destructive. Yet there is a way to be truly self-expressive in the sense of self-perfection. But this is impossible without sacrifice. Incompleteness is always the lot of the undisciplined. To understand this lesson, we turn to Calvary.

When Our Blessed Lord uttered His Fifth Word to the Cross, "I thirst" (*John 19:28)*, a soldier nearby — soldiers are always mentioned kindly in the Scripture — put some wine on a hyssop, and placing it at the end of a long reed reached it to the mouth of Our Blessed Lord, who tasted the wine. The Evangelist adds, "Jesus therefore when he had taken the vinegar said: 'It is consummated" *(John 19:30)*.

Three times this word is used in Sacred Scripture: at the beginning of the world, at the end, and in between. In creation, the Heavens and earth are described as "finished." At the end of the world, a Great Voice is heard coming out of the Temple saying: "It is finished." And now, from the Cross, it is heard again. The word does not mean, "Thank God, it is over." It means it is perfected; the debt had been paid, the work that He had come to do had been completed.

When Mary at the foot of the Cross saw that soldier offer Him wine and heard Him say, "It is consummated," she thought of the moment when it all began. There was wine there too, but not enough. It was the marriage feast of Cana. When in the course of the banquet the wine gave out, the first to observe the lack of wine was not the steward. It was Our Blessed Mother. She notes human needs even before those commissioned to supply them.

Our Blessed Mother said to Our Lord a simple prayer: "They have no wine" *(John 2:3)*. That was all. And her Son answered: "Woman." He did not call her Mother. "Woman, what is that to me and to thee? My hour is not yet come" *(John 2:4)*. Why "Woman"? He was equivalently saying to her: "Mary, you are My Mother. You are asking Me to begin My public life, to declare Myself the Messiah, the Son of God, by working My first miracle. The moment I do that first miracle you cease to be just My Mother. As I reveal myself as Redeemer, you become in a certain sense a co-redemptrix, the Mother of all men. That is why I address you by the title of universal Motherhood: 'Woman.' It will be the beginning of your womanhood."

But what did He mean by saying: "My hour is not yet come?" Our Blessed Lord used that word "hour" often in relation to His Passion and Death. When, for example, His enemies took up stones to throw at Him in the temple, the Evangelist says, "His hour was not yet come" *(John 7:30)*.

The night of the Last Supper, He prayed: "Father, the hour is come. Glorify thy Son, that thy Son may glorify thee" *(John 17:1)*. Then when Judas came out into the Garden, Our Blessed Lord said: "This is your hour" *(Luke 22:53)*. The Hour meant the Cross.

The working of His first miracle was the beginning of the hour. His sixth word from the Cross was the end of that hour. The Passion was finished. The water had been changed into wine; the wine into blood. It is perfected. The work is done.

From these words, the lesson emerges that, between the beginning of our assigned duties and their completion and perfection, there intervenes an "hour," or a moment of mortification, sacrifice, and death. No life is ever finished without it. Between the Cana when we launch the vocation of our lives, and that moment of triumph when we can say we succeeded, there must come the interval of the Cross.

Our Lord could have had no other motive in asking us to take up our cross daily than to perfect ourselves. It was almost like saying, between the day you begin to be a concert pianist and the day you triumph in concert work, there must come the "hour" of hard study, dull exercises, and painful addiction to work.

It is very likely that the reason for the answer Our Lord gave the Greeks when they visited Him: "Unless the grain of wheat falling into the ground die, itself remaineth alone. But if it die, it bringeth forth much fruit" — was to remind them that death is a condition of life. Athens conceivably might have made Him a teacher, but Jerusalem with its Hour would make Him a Redeemer.

The Christ Who is our Head is not a Christ unscarred, but a Christ slain and risen and bearing in His glorified Body the marks of "the Hour" on hands and feet and side. As St. Paul says: "And they that are Christ's have crucified their flesh, with the vices and concupiscences" *(Galatians 5:24).*

Short of this self-discipline by which we humble our pride and restrain our selfishness, our lives are unfinished and incomplete. Most lives are frustrated because they have left out the Cross. They think the endless Day of Eternity can be won without the Crucial Hour of Calvary. Nature abhors incompleteness. Cut off the leg of a salamander, and it will grow another. The impulses we deny in our waking life are often completed in our dreams. Our mutilated souls in one way or another, are trying to complete their incompleteness and to perfect their imperfection.

In the spiritual life this is a conscious, deliberate process: the application of the "Hour" of Christ's Passion to ourselves, that we may share in His Resurrection. "That I may know him and the power of his resurrection and the fellowship of his sufferings: being made conformable to His death" *(Philippians 3:10).*

Our Lord, after rising from the tomb, told the disciples on the way to Emmaus that "the Hour" was the condition of His glory. "O foolish and slow of heart to believe in all things which the prophets have spoken. Ought not Christ to have suffered these things and so to enter his glory?" *(Luke 24:25-26).* Without some systematic detachment on our part, therefore, it is impossible to advance in charity.

The finished man or the perfected man is the non-attached man, non-attached to a craving for power, publicity, and possessions; non-attached to anger, ambition, and avarice; non-attached to selfish desires, lusts, and bodily sensations. The practice of non-attachment to the things which stunt our soul is one of the things meant by "the Hour." It is a going "against the grain"; a being on God's side even against oneself, a renouncement for the sake of recovery.

By what signs will you know whether your life is unfinished? Among others, we mention these: First, the habit of criticism is the best indication of an incomplete life. Our sense of justice is so keen and deep that we do not have it ourselves; we compensate for the lack by trying to make everyone else just. Criticism of others is thus an oblique form of self-commendation. We think we make the picture hang straight on our wall by telling our neighbors that all his pictures are crooked. Like the lark who flutters with great agitation over her nest, we exhibit most flagrantly the very things we seek to hide.

When you say of another's failing, "That is one thing I cannot stand," you reveal the very thing to which you are most unconsciously inclined. We personalize and objectify our unrecognized failings by talking of the failings of others. We hate in others the sins to which we are most likely to be addicted. When Our Lord said, "Judge not, that you may not be judged" *(Matthew 7:1)*, He also meant that you are judged by your judgment of others! You have given yourself away! You are trying to make up for not having the "Hour" by giving others a miserable day.

Another proof of incompleteness is revealed in criticism of religion, either explicit or implicit. If you are a rationalist and regard faith as a superstition, you probably are very fond of ghost stories. You complete your incompleteness by a flight into the incredulous. If you regard all the mysteries of religion as so much worthless superstition, why do you read so many detective stories? You are filling up your need of heavenly mystery with murder mystery.

Why is it that the impure like to read books attacking the purity of others? Why are those who are notoriously undisciplined and unmoral also most contemptuous of religion and morality? They are trying to solace their own unhappy lives by pulling the happy down to their own abysmal depths. They erroneously believe that Bibles and religions, Churches and priests have in some way foisted the distinction between right and wrong in the world and that if they would be done away with, they could go on sinning with impunity. They measure progress by the height of the pile of discarded moral truths.

A third mark of incompleteness is in a state of continual self-reference. The egocentric is always frustrated, simply because the condition of self-perfection is self-surrender. There must be a willingness to die to the lower part of self before there can be a birth to the nobler. That is what Our Lord meant when He said: "For he that will save his life shall lose it; and he that shall lose his life for My sake shall find it" *(Matthew 16:25).*

Many married women who have deliberately spurned the "hour" of childbearing, are unhappy and frustrated. They never discovered the joys of marriage because they refused to surrender to the obligation of their state. In saving themselves, they lost themselves! It takes three to make love, not two: you and you and God. Without God people only succeed in bringing out the worst in each other. Lovers who have nothing else to do but love one another, soon find there is nothing else. Without a central loyalty, life is unfinished.

The youth of America remain juvenile longer than in any other country of the world! The reason is, that so-called "progressive" education by neglecting self-discipline in favor of unbounded self-expression has denied them the one thing that would make them really progressive. To leave out the "hour" of self-renunciation is to make impossible the day of self-development.

It is only by dying to our lower self, that we live to the higher: it is only by surrendering that we control: it is only by crushing our egotism that we can develop our personality. How does the plant get its power to develop? By being unresponsive and unrelated to others, or by surrendering and adjusting itself to its environment that it may survive. How can we enjoy the swim except by surviving the shock of the first cold plunge: how can we enjoy the classics except after the dull routine of grammar? How can we live to the higher life of God unless we make ourselves receptive by self-denial?

Once you have surrendered yourself, you make yourself receptive. In receiving from God, you are perfected and completed. It is a law of nature and grace that only those who give, will ever receive. The Sea of Galilee is fresh and blue and gives life to all the living things within its sunlit waters — not because it receives waters, but because it gives them. The Dead Sea, on the contrary, is dead, simply because it has no outlet. It does not give and, therefore, it never receives. No fish can live in its waters; no beast can thrive upon its shores. Not having had its Calvary of surrender, it never has its Pentecost of Life and Power.

If nothing pleases you, it is because you do not please yourself. If you rarely find a person or thing you like, it is because you do not like yourself. Life does not allow egocentricity to establish its own order, for to life, selfishness is disorder. But how shall this disordered self be oriented to others except by discipline? That is why in the center of the Kingdom of God there is a Cross. (12)

The Seven Words of Jesus and Mary, 1945

PRUDENCE

Behold thy son; behold thy mother.

The greatest crisis in the history of the world was the arrest and conviction of a Man found guilty of no other charge than an excess of love. What was tragic about that crisis reaching from a Garden to a Cross was: Man failed!

Peter, James, and John, who had been given the flashing light of the Transfiguration to prepare them for the dark night of Olives, slept as His enemies attacked. Judas, who had heard the Divine admonition to lay up treasures in Heaven, peddled his Master for thirty pieces of silver -- for Divinity is always sold out of all proportion to due worth.

Peter who had been made the Rock and Key-bearer, warmed himself by a fire and with an atavistic throwback to his fisherman days, cursed and swore to a maidservant that he knew not the man.

As Pilate submitted to the crowd the choice of Christ or a revolutionary upstart, the mob chose Barabbas. Finally, on Calvary where were the men? Where were those whom He cured? Peter was not there, nor his brother Andrew, nor James, nor any of the other Apostles except John, who might not have been there had it not been for the encouragement given him by Mary.

But though men failed in this crisis there is no instance of a single woman failing. In the four trials, the voice heard in His defense was that of a woman, Claudia Procul, the wife of Pontius Pilate, warning her husband not to do anything unjust to that just man. Events proved that the politician was wrong and the woman right.

On the way to Calvary it is the woman who offers consolation, first Veronica wiping away the blood and sweat from His Sacred Face to receive the reward of Its imprint on her towel; then the holy women to whom the Prisoner turned suggesting that only such multiplied mercies and charities as their own could avert catastrophe for their children.

Again on Calvary it is woman who is fearless, for there are several of them at the foot of the Cross. Magdalene, among them as usual, is prostrate. But there is one whose courage and devotion was so remarkable that the Evangelist who was there indicated the detail that she was "standing." That woman was the Mother of the Man on the Central Cross.

When we realize that He who is pinioned to that Cross is the Son of God and therefore possessed of Infinite Wisdom and Power, we are at first inclined to wonder why she should not have been spared the sorrow of Golgotha.

Since He had made her of incomparable beauty of body and soul, why should He not keep those eyes made for Paradise from gazing on a Cross? Why not shield ears attuned to the Divine Word from the blasphemies of ungrateful humans? Since preserved from original sin, why should its penalties be visited upon her? Must Mothers go to gallows with their sons? Must the innocent eat the bitter fruit planted by the sinful?

These are questions of false human wisdom; But God's ways are not our ways. Our Blessed Lord willed her presence there. Since He was the second Adam undoing the sin of the first, Mary would be the new Eve proclaiming the glory of womanhood in the new race of the redeemed.

The woman Eve would not be so cured that her most glorious daughter could not undo her evil. As a woman had shared in the fall of man, so woman should share in his redemption. In no better way could Our Lord reveal woman's role in the new order than by giving John, that disciple whom He loved above the others, to His Mother whom He loved above all: "Son! Behold thy Mother . . . Woman! Behold thy son! "

The Kingdom of God was born! Heavenly prudence had chosen the right means to reveal the new ties born of redemption. Mary was to be our Mother, and we her children.

The Saviour's death was at the same time a birth; the end of a chapter of crucifixion was the beginning of the chapter of a new creation.

As light is instantaneous in dispelling darkness so the Divine Saviour wills that not even a moment shall intervene between breaking down the attachments to Satan by sin and the incorporation of man into the Kingdom of God. She exchanges her Son for the advantages of the Passion and receives its first fruit -- John. He had kept His word: "I will not leave you orphans" *(John 14:18).*

On the Cross was Wisdom Incarnate, dying that we might live. If Our Saviour could have thought of any better means of leading us back to Him, He would have put us in other hands than hers.

There are many falsehoods told about the Catholic Church: One of them is that Catholics adore Mary. This is absolutely untrue. Mary is a creature, human, not Divine. Catholics do not adore Mary. That would be idolatry. But they do reverence her.

And to those Christians who have forgotten Mary, may we ask if it is proper for them to forget her whom He remembered on the Cross? Will they bear no love for that woman through the portals of whose flesh, as the Gate of Heaven, He came to earth?

One of the reasons why so many Christians have lost a belief in the Divinity of Christ is because they lost all affection for her upon whose white body, as a Tower of Ivory, that Infant climbed "to kiss upon her lips a mystic rose."

There is not a Christian in all the world who reverences Mary who does not acknowledge Jesus her Son to be in Truth the Son of the Living God. The prudent Christ on the Cross knew the prudent way to preserve belief in His Divinity, for who better than a Mother knows her son?

The gift of Mary did something to man, for it gave him an ideal love. To fully appreciate this fact dwell for a moment on the difference between two faculties: The intellect, which knows and the will, which loves.

The intellect always whittles down the object to suit itself. That is why the intellect insists on examples, explanations, and analogies. Every teacher must accommodate himself to the mentality of his class, and if the problem, which he is presenting, is abstract and complicated he must break it up into the concrete, as Our Lord described the mysteries of the Kingdom of God in parables.

But the will never works that way. While the intellect pulls down the object of knowledge to its level, the will always goes out to meet the object.

If you love something, you lift yourself up to its level; if you love music you subject yourself to its demands, and if you love mathematics you meet its conditions. We tend to become like that which we love. Boys who love gangsters are already the making of gangsters. As our loves are, that we are. We scale mountains if the object loved is on a mountain; we jump down into the abyss if the object loved is there.

It follows that the higher our loves and ideals, the nobler will be our character. The problem of character training is fundamentally the inculcation of proper ideals. That is why every nation holds up its national heroes, that citizens may become like to them in their patriotism and devotion to country.

If we have heroes and ideal prototypes for those who love sports, the stage, country, army and navy, why should there not be an ideal in the all-important business of leading a good life and saving our souls?

That is precisely one of the roles the Blessed Mother of our Divine Lord plays in Christian life: An object of love so pure, so holy, and so motherly that to be worthy of it we refrain from doing anything which might offend her.

There has hardly ever been a mother in the history of the world who did not at one time or another say to her son or daughter: "Never do anything of which your mother would be ashamed." But what these mothers say is only an echo from the Cross, when Our Divine Lord gave us His Mother as our mother. In giving her to us, He was equivalently saying: "Never do anything of which your Heavenly Mother would be ashamed."

The nobler the love, the nobler the character and what nobler love could be given to men than the woman whom the Saviour of the world chose as His own Mother?

Why is it that the world has confessed its inability to inculcate virtue in the young? Very simply because it has not co-related morality to any love nobler than self-love. Things keep their proportion and fulfill their proper role only when integrated into a larger whole.

Most lives are like doors without hinges, or sleeves without coats, or bows without violins; that is, unrelated to wholes or purposes which give them meaning.

If, for example, a speaker concentrates upon his hands, wonders whether he should put them in his pockets or behind his back it will not be long until he feels he is all hands.

The modern emphasis on sex is a result of tearing a function away from a purpose, a part away from a whole. It can never be handled properly unless integrated to a larger pattern and made to serve it.

That is, to some extent, the role Our Blessed Mother plays in the moral life of our Catholic youth. She is that ideal love for which lesser and baser loves and impulses are sacrificed. Just as a skilled orator so integrates his hands into the pattern of speech that he is never conscious of their presence, so the Catholic youth maintains that healthy self-restraint out of respect for one whom he loves.

The level of any civilization is the level of its womanhood. What they are, men will be, for, to repeat, love always goes out to meet the demands of the object loved. Given a woman like the Mother of Our Lord as our supernatural Mother, you have one of the greatest inspirations for nobler living this world has ever known.

In this hour as never before the world needs to hear again this third word from the Cross. It needs the inspiration of the Good Woman. Unfortunately, the woman who is admired today is not the virtuous woman, but the beautiful woman -- and by beautiful is meant not that inner beauty of the king's daughter, but that beauty which is only skin deep and sometimes only powder deep.

Glance at the advertisements flashed across the pages and billboards of our country! They are for the most part pictures of women who ten years from now would not be accepted for the same advertisement, because they will have lost what they now possess -- a passing beauty.

Our modern world does not really love woman; it loves only her external beauty. If it loved woman, it would love woman as long as she is woman. But because it loves the mask of a woman, it ignores the woman when the mask disappears.

The alarming increase of divorces in our land and the consequent break-up of family life is due principally to the loss of love for the ideal in womanhood. Marriage has become identified with pleasure, not with love. Once the pleasure ceases, love ceases. The woman is loved not for what she is in herself but for what she is to others. The tragedy of such a state is not only what it does for woman, but also what it does for man.

How restore love for woman as *woman*? By giving as the object of life's love a woman who has given Life and Love to the world -- a Woman who is beautiful on the outside all the days of her life, because she is beautiful on the inside. That was the means Our Lord chose on the Cross to remake the world: Remake man by remaking the woman.

Conceived in the Divine Mind, sculptured by the creative fingers of the Heavenly Sculptor, touched by ever radiant color from the palette of heaven, the Artist on the Cross points to His masterpiece and says to man: "Behold the Woman!"

There is told a legend which illustrates the intercessory power of Our Blessed Lady: It seems that one day Our Blessed Lord was walking through the Kingdom of Heaven and saw some souls who had got in very easily. Approaching Peter at the Golden Gate He said: "Peter, I have given to you the keys to the Kingdom of Heaven. You must use your power wisely and discreetly. Tell Me, Peter, how did these souls gain entry into My Kingdom?" To which Peter answered: "Don't blame me, Lord. Every time I close the door, Your Mother opens a window."

When amidst the thousand and one allurements of this world you know not which way to turn, pray to the Woman -- the Virgin most prudent. She knows the true from the false, for in the language of Joyce Kilmer:

At the foot of the Cross on Calvary
Three soldiers sat and diced
And one of them was the devil
And he won the Robe of Christ.

I saw him through a thousand veils
And has not this sufficed?
Now, must I look on the devil robed
In the radiant robe of Christ?

He comes, his face is sad and mild
With thorns his head is crowned
There are great bleeding wounds in His feet
And in each hand a wound.

How can I tell, who am a fool
If this be Christ or no?
Those bleeding hands outstretched to me
Those eyes that love me so!

I see the robe – I look, I hope
I fear – but there is one
Who will direct my troubled mind.
Christ's Mother knows her Son.

O Mother of Good Counsel, lend
Intelligence to me
Encompass me with wisdom
Thou Tower of Ivory!

"This is the man of lies" she says
"Disguised with fearful art:
He has the wounded hands and feet
But not the wounded heart."

Beside the Cross on Calvary
She watched them as they diced
She saw the devil join the game
And win the Robe of Christ.

* From "The Robe of Christ" from Main Street and other poems, by Joyce Kilmer, copyright 1917 by Doubleday, Doran & Company, Inc. (13)

The Seven Virtues, 1940

THE PURPOSE OF LIFE

The Seventh Word from The Cross

"Father, Into Thy Hands I Commend My Spirit." (Luke 23:46)

The Blessed Virgin Mary's Response

"Whatsoever He shall say to you, do ye." (John 2:5)

PROBABLY THE WORD most often used in the contemporary scene is the word *Freedom*. If the sick talk most about health because health is endangered, may it be that the modern talk about freedom means that we are in danger of losing it? It is indeed possible that while we fight to keep our enemies from binding chains to our feet, we become our own enemy by binding chains to our souls.

What I am trying to say is there are two kinds of freedom; a freedom *from* something, and a freedom *for* something; an external freedom from restraints, and an internal freedom of perfection; a freedom to choose evil and a freedom to possess the good.

This inner freedom the typical modern man does not want, because it implies responsibility and, therefore, is a burden — the awful burden of answering, what is the purpose of your life? That is why theories which deny man's inner freedom are so popular today, e.g., Marxism, which destroys freedom in terms of historical determination; Freudianism, which dissolves freedom in the determination of the subconscious and the erotic; totalitarianism, which drowns individual freedom in the totality.

The root of all our trouble is that freedom for God and in God has been interpreted as freedom from God. Freedom is ours to give away. Each of us reveals what we believe to be the purpose of life by the way we use that freedom. For those who would know the supreme purpose of freedom, turn to the life of Our Lord and Our Lady.

The first word Our Lord is recorded as speaking in the Scripture is at the age of twelve: "I must be about my father's business" *(Luke 2:49)*. During His public life, He re-affirmed His obedience to His Father: "I do always the things that please him" *(John 8:29)*. Now on the Cross, when He goes out to meet death and freely surrenders His life, His last words are: "Father, into thy hands I commend my spirit" *(Luke 23:46)*. The last words of other men are spoken in whispers, but He spoke these words in a loud voice.

Death, therefore, did not come to Him; He went to death. No one took His Life away; He laid it down of Himself. He was strong enough to live, but He died by an act of will. This was not an emphasis on dying, but an affirmation of uninterrupted Divine Life. It was the beginning of His return to the glory which He had with the Father before the foundations of the world were laid.

“Father” — note the word of Eternal Parenthood. He did not say "Our Father" as we do, for the Father was not His and ours in the same way. He is the natural Son of the Father; we are only the adopted sons.

“Into Thy Hands" — These were the hands the prophet called "good"; the hands that guided Israel to its historical fulfillment, the hands that provided good things even for the birds of the air and the grass of the field.

"I commend my Spirit" — Surrender! Consecration. Life is a cycle. We come from God, and we go back again to God. Hence the purpose of living is to do God's will.

When Our Blessed Mother saw Him bow His head and deliver His spirit, she remembered that last Word that she ever is recorded to have spoken in Scripture. It was to the wine steward at the marriage feast of Cana: "Whatsoever He shall say to you, do ye" *(John 2:5)*. What a beautiful valedictory! They are the most magnificent words that ever came from the lips of a woman: "Whatsoever He shall say to you, do ye." At the Transfiguration, the Heavenly Father spoke from the Heavens and said: "This is my beloved Son . . . Hear ye him" *(Matthew 17:5)*. Now our Blessed Mother speaks and says, "Do His will."

The sweet relationship of three decades in Nazareth now draws to a close and Mary is about to give Emanuel to us all, and she does it by pointing out to us the one and only way of salvation: complete consecration to her Divine Son. Nowhere in the Scripture is it ever said that Mary loved her son. Words do not prove love. But that love is hidden under the submission of her mind to Him and her final injunction to us: "Whatsoever He shall say to you, do ye."

Both the last recorded word of Jesus and the last recorded word of Mary were words of surrender: Jesus surrendered Himself to the Father; Mary asked us to surrender ourselves to the Son. This is the law of the universe. "For all are yours: And you are Christ's. And Christ is God's" *(1Corinthians 3:22-23)*.

Now face the problem squarely: What do you do with your freedom? You can do three things with it:

1) Keep it for your selfish desires.

2) Break it up into tiny little areas of trivial allegiance or passing fancies.

3) Surrender it to God.

1) If you keep freedom only for yourself, then because it is arbitrary and without standards, you will find it deteriorating into a defiant self-affirmation. Once all things become allowable, simply because you desire them, you become the slave of your choices. If your self-will decides to drink as much as you please, you soon find not only that you are no longer free not to drink, but that you belong to drink and not drink to you. Boundless liberty is boundless tyranny. This is what Our Lord meant when he said: "Whosoever committeth sin is the servant of sin." *(John 8:34)*

(2) The second way out is to become a dilettante, by using your freedom like a hummingbird, hovering first over this flower, then over that, but living for none and dying without any. You desire nothing with all your heart because your heart is broken into a thousand pieces. You thus become divided against yourself; a civil war wages within you, because you swim in contradictory currents.

You change your likes and desires when dissatisfied, but you never change yourself. You are then very much like the man who complained to the cook at breakfast that the egg was not fresh and asked her to bring another. She brought in an egg a minute later, but when he got to the bottom of it, he found it was the same old egg turned upside down. So it is always the same self; what has changed is the desire, not the soul. In that case, even your interest in others is not real.

In your more honest moments, you discover that you have dealt with them on the basis of self-interest; you let them speak when they agree with you, but you silence them when they disagree; even your moments of love are nothing but a barren exchange of egotisms; you talk about yourself five minutes, and he talks about himself five minutes, but if he takes longer he is a bore.

No wonder such people often say: "I must pull myself together." Thus do they confess that they are like broken mirrors, each reflecting a different image. In essence, this is debauchery, or the inability to choose one among many attractions; the soul is diffused, multiple, or "legion" as Satan called himself.

(3) Finally, you can use your freedom as Christ did on the Cross, by surrendering His Spirit to the Father, and as Mary bade us at Cana, by doing His Will in all things. This is perfect freedom: the displacement of self as the center of motivation, and the fixation of our choices, decisions, and actions on Divine Love. "Thy Will be done on earth as it is in Heaven."

We are all like limpets that can live only when they cling to a rock. Our freedom forces us to cling to something. Freedom is ours to give away; we are free to choose our servitudes. To surrender to Perfect Love is to surrender to happiness and thereby be perfectly free.

Thus to "serve Him is to reign." But we are frightened. Like St. Augustine in his early life we say: I want to love you, dear Lord, a little later on, but not now." Fearful of One Who comes to us purple-robed and cypress-crowned, we ask: "Must Thy harvest fields be dunged with rotten death?' Must gold be purified by fire? Must hands that beckon bear the red livid marks of nails? Must I give up my candle, if I have the sun? Must I give up knocking if the door of love is opened? Do we not act toward God and Mary as a child who resents the affectionate embrace of its parents, because it is not our mood to love?

Francis Thompson so reflected when he heard these words from the mouth of a child:

“Why do you so clasp me,

And draw me to your knee?

Forsooth, you do but chafe me,

I pray you let me be:

I will be loved but now and then

When it liketh me!’

So I heard a young child,

A thwart child, a young child

Rebellious against love’s arms,

Make its peevish cry.

To the tender God I turn: —

‘Pardon, Love most High!

For I think those arms were even Thine,

And that child even I.”

As Pascal said: "There are only two kinds of people we can call reasonable: either those who serve God with their whole heart because they know Him, or those who search after Him with all their heart because they do not know Him."

There is, therefore, some hope for those who are dissatisfied with their choices, and who want. If you do just that, you create a void. Far better it is for you to say: "I am a sinner," than to say: "I have no need of religion." The empty can be filled, but the self-intoxicated have no room for God. Could we but make the surrender, we would cry out with Augustine "Too late, O ancient Beauty, have I loved Thee," as we have discovered in the language of the great poet:

"O gain that lurk'st ungained in all gain!
O love we just fall short of in all love!
O height that in all heights art still above!
O beauty that dost leave all beauty pain!
Thou unpossessed that mak'st possession vain." (14)

The Seven Words of Jesus and Mary, 1945

THE SELFISH

The third group in the world who need to feel the impact of the Cross are the selfish. By the selfish is here understood all those who feel that salvation is either an individual matter or else the concern of a particular class; that religion has no other right to exist than to remove the impediments of a selfish existence by slum clearance, social security, more playgrounds; and that all else, such as the regeneration of man from sin, or the culture of the soul, is a snare and a delusion.

When the selfish become learned they define religion, in the language of a contemporary philosopher, as "what a man does with his own solitariness"; when the selfish are in distress, they ask "why should God do this to me?" when the selfish sin, they say, "What harm does my sin do to anyone else?"

The selfish were on Calvary's hill in their representative who was the thief on the left! He had heard the blasphemy and pride of his companion thief broken, when out of a consciousness of sin he called to the Lord for mercy; but the experience left him untouched. One can be so close to God physically, and yet miss Him spiritually.

Turning to the Lord on the Central Cross, the thief on the left, in the supreme expression of selfishness, cried out with bitterness of soul: "If thou be Christ, save thyself and us" *(Luke 23:29)*.

He was the first Marxist! Long before Marx, he was saying "Religion is the opium of the people."

A religion that thinks only of souls when men are dying, which bids them look to God at the moment when the courts are inflicting injustice, which talks about "pie in the sky" when stomachs are empty and bodies racked with pain, which talks about forgiveness when the social outcasts -- two thieves and a despised proletarian, a village carpenter -- are dying on a scaffold, is a religion that is the opium of the people.

"Save thyself and us" -- How modern! Salvation is for a class! Not everyone! Communism speaks only for the proletariat: "Save thyself and us." Fascism speaks only for the nation: "Save thyself and us." Nazism speaks only for the race: "Save thyself and us." The rich speak only for their class: "Save thyself and us."

Not a word about the salvation of the world, about His people whom He loved, about the Gentiles to whom He would send His Apostles; and above all else, not a word about His beloved Mother beneath His cross whose heart was already pierced by seven swords.

If there was to be salvation for the thief on the left it was not to be spiritual or moral, but physical: "Save thyself and us!" Save what? Our souls? No! Man has no soul! Save our bodies! What good is religion if it cannot stop pain, step down from a gibbet, rescue a class, or pamper selfish interests? Christianity is either a social gospel or it is a drug.

Our Lord did not answer that selfish thief directly, but He did answer Him indirectly when, looking down from the Cross, He addressed Himself to the two most beloved creatures on earth -- Mary, His Mother, and John, His Disciple. But He did not address them as "Mary" and as "John."

If He had called them by their names, they would have remained what they were; representatives of a certain class. If He had said "Mother," she would have been His Mother and no one else's. If he had said "John," he would have been the son of Zebedee, and the son of no one else. So He called Mary "Woman" and John "Son." "Woman, behold thy son . . . son behold thy mother" *(John 19:26-27)*.

He was saying that religion is not what a man does with his solitariness, but what he does with his relationships. And as if to prove for all time that religion is not selfishness, either of an individual or a "set" or a class, He called Mary and John into a relationship as wide as the world. In a certain sense He de-classified them.

She was no longer to be His Mother alone. As He was the new Adam, she would be the new Eve. He had told her about a year and a half before that there were other ties than those of flesh and blood, namely, the spiritual bond among those who do the will of God. "Behold my mother and my brethren. For whosoever shall do the will of God, he is my brother, and my sister and mother" *(Mark 3:34-35)*.

Now He establishes that new relationship. As she was His Mother by the flesh, she would now be the mother of all "who are born, not of blood, nor of the will of the flesh, nor of the will of man, but of God" *(John 1:13)*.

To herald her in this new relationship as the Mother of Christians, He calls her "Woman" -- it was a high summons to universal motherhood.

And John, who up to this point is the son of Zebedee, is not called John -- for that would have been to keep the ties of blood. He is addressed as "Son." "son, behold thy mother."

Jesus was the first born of Mary's flesh, but John was the first born of her Spirit at the foot of the Cross; and perhaps Peter was the second, Andrew the third, James the fourth, and we the millionth and millionth born.

He was setting up a new family, a new social relationship. In that context, economic and social questions would be settled, and not otherwise. "Seek ye first the kingdom of God and his justice, and all these things shall be added unto you" *(Luke 12:31).*

Religion is not an individual affair! A man can no more have an individual religion than he can have an individual government or an individual astronomy or mathematics. Religion is social, and so social is it that it is not limited to the criminal class, as the thief believed, not to any class, race, nation, or color. All these views are too aristocratic.

Snobbery can exist among proletarians as well as among dukes. The new totalitarian systems have produced "blue bloods" just as obnoxious as some of the blue bloods of monarchy.

This word of Our Lord furthermore reveals that all social duties flow out of these spiritual relationships. He did not say: "John, take care of My Mother," nor did He say: "Mary, look after John as you would me." No! Having established a new relationship between Mary and John, namely that of motherhood and sonship, the duties flowed quite naturally.

Religion is made the sharing of responsibilities. Mary had raised her Child, but now she was to adopt others and love them as sons, poor indeed though they were in comparison.

John had fulfilled his sonship to Zebedee, but now he was to take on new duties as her son and so live that he would never do anything of which his Mother would be ashamed.

Mary continued her duty of bearing the burden of others, for we find her on Pentecost in the midst of the Apostles, mothering the Infant Church as she mothered the Infant Jesus.

John too could never forget that word "son" which he heard from the Cross, as we find him some years after the Ascension writing to the Infant Church: "Behold what manner of charity the Father hath bestowed upon us, that we should be called, and should be the sons of God" *(1John 3:1).*

There is no Messianic race, no Messianic class, no Messianic color. Our Lord died for all men, and thus set up a new series of relationships with God. And from out of this new set of relationships, slum clearance and social justice and all the rest *follow* -- but not otherwise.

Hence Our Blessed Lord said nothing about slavery, because He knew that slavery would never be eradicated until men saw themselves related to one another on the basis of equality as children of God.

He did not discourse on the need of child clinics. He first proclaimed the value of a child to a pagan world by becoming a child among children.

He said nothing about the necessity of democracy. But He laid the foundation for it, when He told Pilate what we, over 1700 years later, wrote in the Declaration of Independence -- that all rights and liberties come from God.

He said nothing about the rights of labor. He first dignified it as a vocation by working as a carpenter.

He said nothing about treating servants decently, but He girded Himself with a towel and washed the feet of His own Apostles. "And whosoever will be first among you, shall be the servant of all" *(Mark 10:44)*.

The classic example of the effect of the new relationship was the slave Onesimus, who ran away from his master Philemon. The slave came to Paul who made him a Christian. Paul then asked the slave to return to Philemon bearing a note in which Onesimus is called "my own son whom I have begotten in my bands. . . Do thou receive him as my own . . Receive him . . . not now as a servant . . . but a most dear brother especially to me; but how much more to thee, both in the flesh and in the Lord' *(Philemon 1:10-16)*. He was no longer a slave, because he was a Christian.

What barriers St. Paul would have broken down in his League of Nations: "There is neither Jew nor Greek" (that means, no race or political distinction); "there is neither bond nor free" (no economic distinction);

"there is neither male nor female" (no sex distinction); "for you are all one in Christ Jesus" *(Galatians 3:28)*.

When Chile and Argentina were about to go to war, it was the suggestion of a woman that the cannon of the two nations be melted, made into a statue of Christ and placed in the Andes at the border of each and be called "The Christ of the Andes." And it bears this inscription: "Sooner shall these mountains crumble than this pact of peace, entered into at the feet of Christ between these two nations, shall be broken." And that pact has never been broken!

Some day someone will read the Gospel: "Thou shalt love thy neighbor as thyself"; that is, love the other's interest as you do self interest Not until all groups see themselves as bound in a new relationship to the common good, will they sacrifice their own special interests.

So long as every individual exists for himself, we shall have social discontent; so long as every class seeks only its own interest we shall have class warfare; and so long as each nation seeks its own interest exclusively, we shall have war.

After listening to that third word to the Cross we know that the equal distribution of economic goods does not make men brothers, but that, by making men brothers under the Fatherhood of God, economic goods are distributed. Equality of possessions does not make men brothers; but being brothers makes for economic equality.

The Prodigal Son thought he could have peace through distribution of economic wealth, but it was not until he had restored relations with his father that the distribution worked.

Communism of things will never work until we start with a communism of personal relationships. Individual selfishness cannot be corrected by class selfishness. Selfishness is insanity.

The author of Peer Gynt writes of the inmates of an insane asylum: "It is here that men are most themselves -- themselves and nothing but themselves -- sailing with outspread wings of self. Each shuts himself in a cask of self, the cask stopped with the bung of self and seasoned in a well of self. None has a tear for the other's woes or cares what any other thinks."

Centering on self, they hate themselves. Doing always what they like, they hate what they do. Having their own way, they block the way and lose their way. Unable to get along with themselves, they cannot get along with anyone else.

No wonder a young product of a progressive school once asked: "Must I always do what I want to do?" It is by no accident that this age which believed in self-expression has ended in self-disillusionment and disgust.

Our Lord spoke to the hating, raging, anti-Christian Saul on the Damascus road: "Saul, Saul, why persecutest thou me? It is hard for thee to kick against the goad" *(Acts 26:14)*. He used the figure of an ox hurting itself by kicking against the sharp nails of the cart. He was saying in effect:

"When you rebel against Me, you are rebelling against yourself . . . You persecute Me, but you -- *you* are perishing."

Men, nations and systems always destroy themselves by seeking an order other than that based on the brotherhood of all men under the Fatherhood of God! Class consciousness must be transformed into "brother consciousness," or the world will perish. Freedom from God is really the freedom to destroy ourselves.

To the selfish comes the lesson from the Cross! Begin to live for others, and you will begin to live for self. Religion implies social relationships.

We did not wait until we were twenty-one and then, after studying the Constitution, decide to become Americans. We were born American -- born out of the womb of America. So likewise, in the spiritual order, we are born out of the womb of the Church. It is the Church founded by Christ which makes us Christian; it is not you or me, as a Christian, who adds our individuality to other individuals to form an institution!

Never therefore say: Religion is a purely personal matter. You can no more have your personal religion than you can have your personal sun. If your personal religion unites you to God, and my personal religion unites me to God, then is there not a common relationship between us to a common Father?

When we go to a concert, do we not give attention to the music, that is, do we not allow ourselves to be determined by something *outside* ourselves? Do we think that when people attend concerts, each one should do whatever he pleases, call out his own selections, take the baton from the conductor, or whistle his own tune?

Then why, when the subject is religion, where the Conductor is God, should we insist on our own individual ideas, or say religion is "what I think about God." Rather, religion is what God wants it to be, hence I must seek His will, not mine, discover His truth, not my opinion.

Nor is it true to say: "The way I conduct my own life is nobody's business but mine," or "it harms nobody else." Could you throw a stone in the sea without causing ripples which would affect even the most distant shore? How then do we think our moral actions can be devoid of social repercussions?

Morality is essentially a relationship of a threefold character: a relationship between my self and my conscience, between my self and my neighbor, and between my self and my God.

You cannot think of a single wrong deed in the world which does not disturb all three relationships -- even secret sins. Take, for example, a strong hatred which never expresses itself in violence.

First, it disturbs your relation to yourself; physically, by upsetting your stomach, spiritually by creating a tension between an ideal and a failure to attain it, and morally, later on, by remorse of conscience.

Secondly it disturbs your relation to your neighbor, by diminishing the content of love in the world. And if enough individuals did exactly what you did, it could cause a war.

Thirdly, it disturbs your relation to God, for if I am a motor made by God which runs best on the fuel of Divine Love which God supplies, it follows that I upset both myself and my happy relation to Him by trying to run the motor on the fuel of hate.

All quarrels, disagreements, wars, strifes, and dissensions begin with a false declaration of independence -- independence from God and independence from fellowman.

That incidentally is why the Jews on the one hand, and the Christians on the other, are on the wrong track when they try to break down intolerance by protests within their own group.

The Jews will never crush anti-Semitism so long as they protest against intolerance only within their ranks, or within their press, and completely ignore the intolerance shown to Christians. And the same is true of Christians. Not until they both protest out of a common relationship, until the Jew defends the Christian and the Christian the Jew, will there be peace.

One of the reasons why there has been such a great decline of belief in the Divinity of Christ outside the Church is because a proper understanding of the relationship existing between Christ and His Mother has been destroyed.

Would you, as a son, have much regard for anyone who said he liked you, but who refused to speak to your mother? Well, do you think Our Lord can feel any differently, particularly since He gave His Mother to us on the Cross?

Why not then, as a remedy for all selfishness, begin seeing ourselves bound to one another in every increasing relationship, first as common creatures of God, then as sons of the Heavenly Father, as brothers of Christ, as members of His Mystical Body vivified by one Spirit, governed by one Head, and as children of Mary, Our Mother, to whom -- as her children who never grow up -- we say in the language of Mary Dixon Thayer:

Lovely Lady dressed in Blue
Teach me how to pray!
God was just your little Boy,
Tell me what to say!

Did you lift Him up, sometimes,
Gently, on your knee?
Did you sing to Him the way
Mother does to me?

Did you hold His hand at night?
Did you ever try
Telling stories of the world?
O! And did He cry?

Do you really think He cares
If I tell Him things --
Little things that happen? And
Do the Angel's wings

Make a noise? And can He hear
Me if I speak low?
Does He understand me now?
Tell me for you know!

Lovely Lady dressed in Blue.
Teach me how to pray!
God was just your little Boy,
And you know the way.

(From A Child on His Knees – c/o Macmillan Co., New York) [15]

Seven Words to the Cross, 1944

WHEN CALVARY BECOMES THE NURSERY

HAVE YOU EVER wondered what it means to be a child of God? The Catechism of the Catholic Church teaches us that through baptism, we become "an adopted child of God, who has become a partaker of the divine nature, member of Christ and co-heir with him, and a temple of the Holy Spirit." (CCCC 1265)

Similarly, the Church teaches us that when Our Blessed Lord spoke these words from the Cross: "Woman behold your son, Son behold your Mother" (Jn. 19:26), that we were given at that moment, the title, 'Children of Mary.'

To help flesh out this teaching on spiritual adoption in a deeper way, we will once again ponder some of the words shared by Archbishop Sheen earlier in this book.

"An angel of light went out and came to where a humble virgin of Nazareth knelt in prayer, and said, "Hail, full of grace!" These were not words; they were the Word. "And the Word became flesh." This was the first Annunciation.

Nine months passed and once more an angel from that great white Throne of Light came down to shepherds on Judean hills, teaching them the joy of a "Gloria in Excelsis," and bidding them worship Him Whom the world could not contain, a "Babe wrapped in swaddling clothes and laid in a manger." Eternity became time, Divinity incarnate, God a man; Omnipotence was discovered in bonds. In the language of Saint Luke,

Mary "brought forth her firstborn Son . . .and laid Him in a manger." This was the first Nativity.

Then came Nazareth and the carpenter shop where one can imagine the Divine Boy, straitened until baptized with a baptism of blood, fashioning a little cross in anticipation of a great Cross that would one day be His on Calvary. One can also imagine Him in the evening of a day of labor at the bench, stretching out His arms in exhausted relaxation, while the setting sun traced on the opposite wall the shadow of a man on a cross. One can, too, imagine His Mother seeing in each nail the prophecy and the telltale of a day when men would carpenter to a Cross the One who carpentered the universe.

Nazareth passed into Calvary, and the nails of the shop into the nails of human malignity. From the Cross He completed His last will and testament. He had already committed His blood to the Church, His garments to His enemies, a thief to Paradise, and would soon commend His body to the grave and His soul to His Heavenly Father. To whom, then, could He give the two treasures which He loved above all others, Mary and John? He would bequeath them to one another, giving at once a son to His Mother and a Mother to His friend. "Woman!" It was the second Annunciation! The midnight hour, the silent room, the ecstatic prayer had given way to the mount of Calvary, the darkened sky, and a Son hanging on a Cross. Yet, what consolation! It was only an angel who made the first Annunciation, but it is God's own sweet voice, which makes the second.

"Behold your son!" It was the second Nativity! Mary had brought forth her First-born without labor, in the cave of Bethlehem; she now brings forth her second-born, John, in the labors of the Cross. At this moment Mary is undergoing the pains of childbirth, not only for her second-born, who is John, but also for the millions who will be born to her in Christian ages as 'Children of Mary'. Now we can understand why Christ was called 'her First-born'. It was not because she was to have other children by the blood of flesh, but because she was to have other children by the blood of her heart. Truly, indeed, the Divine condemnation against Eve is now renewed against the new Eve, Mary, for she is bringing forth her children in sorrow.

Mary, then, is not only the Mother of Our Lord and Savior, Jesus Christ, but she is also our Mother, and this not by a title of courtesy, not by legal fiction, not by a mere figure of speech, but by the right of bringing us forth in sorrow at the foot of the Cross. It was by weakness and disobedience at the foot of the tree of Good and Evil that Eve lost the title, Mother of the Living; it is at the foot of the tree of the Cross that Mary, by sacrifice and obedience, regained for us the title, Mother of the Living. What a destiny to have the Mother of God as my Mother and Jesus as my Brother (16)

Oh, the joy that can come in accepting this profound reality that Mary is our Mother and Jesus is our Brother. What a tremendous gift we have received from God the Father! But what does this gift entail? Our Blessed Lord gave us His Mother from His Cross on Calvary but what are our responsibilities to her? And what are her responsibilities to us?

The Catholic Church teaches that when we die, we will be judged by Christ and will have to make an accounting of lives. Some of us may wonder what questions God will ask of us. Did I feed the poor? Did I avoid sin? Did I make peace instead of war? But what if I told you that one of the questions Jesus might ask us would be:

"Did You Love My Mother?"

Now for me, pondering this question has caused me many a restless night. To be honest, I had ignored Mary for many years. I had given her lip service, with a few half-hearted rosaries and novenas. I had been guilty of saying that Mary was my Mother — but in name only. In actual fact, I was not allowing Mary to be my Mother.

With time I started to think, did not Christ desire to share with me His Kingdom and all its treasures? Why would I choose to ignore the one person that God chose to be His Mother and mine? Why would I choose to reject the love, guidance, graces, and blessing that the Blessed Mother wanted to give me, as she certainly gave Our Lord during His life?

Well, after searching my heart and taking stock of what I had done and what I had failed to do with regards to the Blessed Mother, I truly started to experience a sense of sorrow. I knew that I needed somehow to apologize in some way to the Blessed Virgin Mary. But sadly, this apology would take a while to materialize because, as you might know, sometimes the three hardest words to say in life are: "**I am sorry!**" Fortunately for me, by God's grace and Our Lady's intercession, I eventually apologized to the Blessed Mother. But that apology came after a real-life situation, provided me with a kind of 'epiphany.'

A Reckless One

We all know stories of drunk drivers who get behind the wheel of a car and kill innocent people. Sadly, this story is repeated time and time again. There are casualties on both sides of these tragic stories: the families devastated by their loss and the drivers who have to live with the consequences of their bad decisions.

With this thought, I started to ask myself, how would I respond if a drunk driver asked me for mercy after killing my child? For some strange coincidence, while I was pondering on this thought, I saw out of the corner of my eye, a crucifix hanging on the wall in my living room. As I looked upon it for a few moments, my epiphany came to me. At that moment, I saw the connection between the drunk driver killing an innocent victim with his car and the stark reality that it was my sins that caused the death of an innocent victim, Jesus Christ, who had to pay for my sins by dying on the Cross.

I had realized that it was my sin that nailed Jesus to His Cross. I was guilty of His death. I was the reckless one that now needed to apologize to the Victim's Mother for the role that I played in the death of her Son. That victim was Jesus, and the Mother of the victim was the Blessed Virgin Mary.

But how does one apologize to the Blessed Mother? Let me share a few words from Archbishop Sheen that will help.

He writes, "If you can stand the gaze of a Crucifix long enough, you will discover these truths. First, if sin cost Him Who is Innocence, so much, then I who am guilty cannot take it lightly; second, in all the world, there is only one thing worse than sin, and that is to forget I am a sinner; third, more bitter than the Crucifixion must be my rejection of that Love by which I was redeemed." (17)

"There is no escaping the one thing necessary in the Christian life, namely saving our souls and purchasing the glorious liberty of the children of God. The crucifixion ends, but Christ endures. Sorrows pass, but we remain. Therefore we must never come down from the supreme end and purpose of life, the salvation of our souls." (12)

“What had she done to deserve the Seven Swords? What crimes had she committed to robbing her of her Son? She had done nothing, but we have. We have sinned against her Divine Son, we have sentenced him to the Cross, and in sinning against him we wounded her.

In fact, we thrust into her hands the greatest of all griefs, for she was not losing a brother, or a sister, or a father, or a mother, or even just a son -- she was losing God. And what greater sorrow is there than this!

Finally, we should mourn for the greatest of all reasons, namely, because of what our sins have done to him. If we had been less proud, his crown of thorns would have been less piercing; if we had been less avaricious, the nails in the hands would have been less burning; if we had traveled less in the devious ways of sin, his feet would not have been so deeply dug with steel; if our speech had been less biting, his lips would have been less parched; if we had been less sinful, his agony would have been shorter; if we had loved more, he would have been hated less.” (18)

It may be difficult, but may I encourage you to take a moment to reflect on your relationship with the Blessed Mother and to see if an apology might be in order? Just imagine yourself approaching her at the foot of the cross with St. Mary Magdalene weeping on her knees beside her and St. John standing there with you. Look up to our Crucified Lord and then take a few moments to reflect on His death. Then, may I encourage you to reach out as I did and apologize to the Blessed Mother for the role you played in the death of her Son.

I recall a song written in 2001 by Fr. Eugene O’Reilly, CSsR. The song was entitled ‘Father I Have Sinned’ (The Prodigal Son). The lyrics are beautiful and provide great consolation to many ‘prodigals’ like myself.

Having made my confession and asking for pardon, I envisioned the Blessed Mother singing the words of the chorus in that beautiful song: *I forgive you. I love you. You are mine. Take my hand. Go in peace, sin no more, beloved one.*

For myself, I knew at once, that when I made my apology to the Blessed Mother, my life changed; my relationship with her was strengthened. I rejoiced in thinking how great her joy would be, to shelter under her mantle, one more of her Son's lost sheep!

Our Mother, Our Champion

I will leave you this one last pearl of wisdom from Archbishop Sheen:

"May I recommend that if you have never before prayed to Mary, do so now. Can you not see that if Christ himself willed to be physically formed in her for nine months and then be spiritually formed by her for thirty years. It is to her that we must go to learn how to have Christ formed in us? Only she who raised Christ can raise a Christian.

"There are many falsehoods told about the Catholic Church: One of them is that Catholics adore Mary. This is absolutely untrue. Mary is a creature, human, not divine. Catholics do not adore Mary. That would be idolatry But they do reverence her.

And to those Christians who have forgotten Mary, may we ask if it is proper for them to forget her whom He remembered on the Cross? Will they bear no love for that woman through the portals of whose flesh, as the Gate of Heaven, He came to earth?

One of the reasons why so many Christians have lost a belief in the Divinity of Christ is because they lost all affection for her upon whose white body, as a Tower of Ivory, that Infant climbed "to kiss upon her lips a mystic rose."

There is not a Christian in the entire world that reverences Mary, who does not acknowledge Jesus her Son to be in Truth, the Son of the Living God. The prudent Christ on the Cross, knew the prudent way to preserve belief in His Divinity, for whom better than a Mother knows her son?" (21)

"And now at the end of his life, the Roman governor could say: "Your own nation...has delivered you up to me." Thus did he who is King of Kings become socially poor and an outcast from the snobs of the earth, in order that through that abandonment we might become -- let us pause at the very thought of it -- children of God!" (22)

"There is no stopping it except by reversing the process by which we drove God out of the world, namely by relighting the lamp of faith in the souls of men." (23)

"His soul that was burning and His Heart that was on fire. He was thirsting for the souls of men. The Shepherd was lonely without His sheep; the Creator was yearning for His creatures; the First-born was looking for His brethren." (24)

Christ is waiting for our response. Our Brother Christ, who is also our Lord and our God, waits at the side of our crib, in the nursery called Calvary He presents to us His Mother as our loving helper. He keeps good His promise "I shall not leave you orphaned".

Christ said, "My sheep hear my voice. I know them, and they follow me." The Good Lord knows each one of us and he knows His Mother. Think of how much easier it will be for those souls, who like the Apostle John, 'took Mary into their home'. The calming effect of a Mother; the blessing; the encouragement; the companionship and the fellowship that John experienced by being obedient to Christ's words, "Behold your Mother", these are the graces that await us, her children.

When we read the scriptures, we see that the Virgin Mary and Christ are inseparable. Wherever Our Lord is mentioned, she is found there near Him. When Christ comes again in glory and searches for his sheep, would it not be easier for Him to find us if His Mother has taken up residence with us and she is by our side? What a great advocate and companion we will have on that day when we are reunited with our Brother and Lord.

Let us not be afraid to take Mary into our home, and to accept the adoption that God has arranged for us at the foot of Calvary.

Calvary has truly become a nursery and each one of us has been given three special gifts at the foot of the Cross. The first is the Blessed Virgin Mary who has become our Mother. The second is our own crib. And the third is our own cross.

Please know that there are many cribs in this nursery alongside yours. Our Blessed Mother Mary is there to care for us and to lead us to our Saviour, for we do not save our souls alone, but only in companionship with others.

Each of us, too, has a cross. Our Lord said: "If any man will follow me" *(Mark 8:34)*. He did not say: "Take up my cross." My cross is not the same as yours, and yours is not the same as mine. Every cross in the world is tailor made, custom built, patterned to fit one and no one else.

That is why we say: "My cross is hard." We assume that other persons' crosses are lighter, forgetful that the only reason our cross is hard is simply that it is our own. Our Lord did not make His Cross; it was made for Him. So yours is made by the circumstances of your life, and by your routine duties. That is why it fits so tightly. Crosses are not made by machines but by God.

I pray that this journey of discovery given by Archbishop Fulton J. Sheen has touched your heart. Each of us has a cross to carry and a crib to rest in.

Hopefully, there will be times in our lives when we will look up from our cribs and thank the Good Lord for all that He has done for us and the many opportunities he has given to us to love Him and Our Blessed Mother.

Remember that the cribs of God's children are located at the foot of the Cross. May we be so blessed to look upon the cross each day from our cribs and remember the love that Jesus Christ has for us in that he laid down his life for us on the Cross.

Let us not be afraid to fully embrace the spiritual adoption that God has arranged for us at the foot of Calvary, to become 'Children of Mary.'

And may those sweet words of our Blessed Lord "Behold Thy Mother" be that gentle reminder that you are not alone and that you belong to the family of God.

Permit me to close with a short, childlike prayer I often say through the day:

"Jesus, Mary, and Joseph, I Love You! Never leave me! Please save souls, including my own! Amen."

God Love You.

Allan Smith

ACKNOWLEDGMENTS

To the members of the Archbishop Fulton John Sheen Foundation in Peoria, Illinois. In particular, to the Most Rev. Daniel R. Jenky, C.S.C., Bishop of Peoria, for your leadership and fidelity to the cause of Sheen's canonization and the creation of this book.

www.archbishopsheencause.org

To the staff at Sophia Institute Press for their invaluable assistance in sharing the writings of Archbishop Fulton J. Sheen to a new generation of readers.

www.sophiainstitute.com

To the volunteers at the Archbishop Fulton J. Sheen Mission Society of Canada: your motto "Unless Souls are Saved, Nothing is Saved", speaks to the reality that Jesus Christ came into the world to make salvation available to all souls.

www.archbishopfultonjsheenmissionsocietyofcanada.org

To the good folks at 'Bishop Sheen Today'. We value your guidance, support, and prayers in helping us to share the wisdom of Archbishop Fulton J. Sheen. Your apostolic work of sharing his audio and video presentations along with his many writings to a worldwide audience is very much appreciated.

www.bishopsheentoday.com

And lastly, to Archbishop Fulton J. Sheen, whose teachings on Our Lord's Passion and His Seven Last Words continue to inspire me to love God more and to appreciate the gift of the Church. May we be so blessed as to imitate Archbishop Sheen's love for the saints, the sacraments, the Eucharist, and the Blessed Virgin Mary. May the Good Lord grant him a very high place in heaven!

ABOUT THE AUTHOR

Fulton J. Sheen

(1895–1979)

ARCHBISHOP SHEEN, best known for his popularly televised and syndicated television program, Life is Worth Living, is held today as one of Catholicism's most widely recognized figures of the twentieth century.

Fulton John Sheen, born May 8, 1895, in El Paso, Illinois was raised and educated in the Roman Catholic faith. Originally named Peter John Sheen, he came to be known as a young boy by his mother's maiden name, Fulton. He was ordained a priest of the Diocese of Peoria at St. Mary's Cathedral in Peoria, IL on September 20, 1919.

Following his ordination, Sheen studied at the Catholic University of Louvain, where he earned a doctorate in philosophy in 1923. That same year, he received the Cardinal Mercier Prize for International Philosophy, becoming the first-ever American to earn this distinction.

Upon returning to America, after varied and extensive work throughout Europe, Sheen continued to preach and teach theology and philosophy from 1927 to 1950, at the Catholic University of America in Washington DC.

Beginning in 1930, Sheen hosted a weekly Sunday night radio broadcast called 'The Catholic Hour'. This broadcast captured many devoted listeners, reportedly drawing an audience of four million people every week for over twenty years.

In 1950, he became the National Director of the Society for the Propagation of the Faith, raising funds to support missionaries. During the sixteen years that he held this position, millions of dollars were raised to support the missionary activity of the Church. These efforts influenced tens of millions of people all over the world, bringing them to know Christ and his Church. In addition, his preaching and personal example brought about many converts to Catholicism.

In 1951, Sheen was appointed Auxiliary Bishop of the Archdiocese of New York. That same year, he began hosting his television program 'Life is Worth Living', which lasted for six years.

In the course of its run, that program competed for airtime with popular television programs hosted by the likes of Frank Sinatra and Milton Berle. Sheen's program held its own, and in 1953, just two years after its debut, he won an Emmy Award for "Most Outstanding Television Personality." Fulton Sheen credited the Gospel writers - Matthew, Mark, Luke, and John - for their valuable contribution to his success. Sheen's television show ran until 1957, boasting as many as thirty million weekly viewers.

In the Fall of 1966, Sheen was appointed Bishop of Rochester, New York. During that time, Bishop Sheen hosted another television series, 'The Fulton Sheen Program' which ran from 1961 to 1968, closely modeling the format of his 'Life is Worth Living' series.

After nearly three years as Bishop of Rochester, Fulton Sheen resigned and was soon appointed by Pope Paul VI as Titular Archbishop of the See of Newport, Wales. This new appointment allowed Sheen the flexibility to continue preaching.

Another claim to fame was Bishop Sheen's annual Good Friday homilies, which he preached for fifty-eight consecutive years at St. Patrick's Cathedral in New York City, and elsewhere. Sheen also led numerous retreats for priests and religious, preaching at conferences all over the world.

When asked by Pope St. Pius XII how many converts he had made, Sheen responded, "Your Holiness, I have never counted them. I am always afraid that if I did count them, I might think I made them, instead of the Lord."

Sheen was known for being approachable and down to earth. He used to say, "If you want people to stay as they are, tell them what they want to hear. If you want to improve them, tell them what they should know." This he did, not only in his preaching but also through his numerous books and articles. His book titled 'Peace of Soul' was sixth on the New York Times best-seller list.

Three of Sheen's great loves were: the missions and the propagation of the faith; the Holy Mother of God and the Eucharist.

He made a daily holy hour of prayer before the Blessed Sacrament. It was from Jesus Himself that he drew strength and inspiration to preach the gospel, and in the Presence of Whom that he prepared his homilies. "I beg [Christ] every day to keep me strong physically and alert mentally, in order to preach His gospel and proclaim His Cross and Resurrection," he said. "I am so happy doing this that I sometimes feel that when I come to the good Lord in Heaven, I will take a few days' rest and then ask Him to allow me to come back again to this earth to do some more work."

His contributions to the Catholic Church are numerous and varied, ranging from educating in classrooms, churches, and homes, to preaching over a nationally-publicized radio show, and two television programs, as well as penning over sixty written works. Archbishop Fulton J. Sheen had a gift for communicating the Word of God in the most pure, simple way. His strong background in philosophy helped him to relate to everyone in a highly personalized manner. His timeless messages continue to have great relevance today. His goal was to inspire everyone to live a God-centered life with the joy and love that God intended.

On October 2, 1979, Archbishop Sheen received his greatest accolade, when Pope St. John Paul II embraced him at St. Patrick's Cathedral in New York City. The Holy Father said to him, "You have written and spoken well of the Lord Jesus. You are a loyal son of the Church."

The good Lord called Fulton Sheen home on December 9, 1979. His television broadcasts now available through various media, and his books, extend his earthly work of winning souls for Christ.

Sheen's cause for canonization was opened in 2002. In 2012, Pope Benedict XVI declared him 'Venerable', and in July of 2019, Pope Francis formally approved the miracle necessary for Sheen's beatification and canonization process to move forward. The time and date for the church to declare Archbishop Fulton J. Sheen a saint is in God's hands.

BIBLIOGRAPHY NOTES

WOMAN, BEHOLD THY SON - Fulton J. Sheen, The Seven Last Words – (New York: Century Co. Ltd., 1933).

THE VALUE OF IGNORANCE - Fulton J. Sheen, Seven Words of Jesus and Mary - (New York: P.J. Kenedy & Sons, 1945).

THY KINGDOM COME - Fulton J. Sheen, The Fullness of Christ – (Huntington, IN: Our Sunday Visitor, 1935).

THE SECRET OF SANCTITY - Fulton J. Sheen, Seven Words of Jesus and Mary - (New York: P.J. Kenedy & Sons, 1945).

THE SANCTUS - Fulton J. Sheen, Calvary And The Mass – (New York: P.J. Kenedy & Sons, 1936).

THE FELLOWSHIP OF RELIGION - Fulton J. Sheen, Seven Words of Jesus and Mary - (New York: P.J. Kenedy & Sons, 1945).

BLESSED ARE THE CLEAN OF HEART - Fulton J. Sheen, The Cross and The Beatitudes - (New York: P.J. Kenedy & Sons, 1937).

CONFIDENCE IN VICTORY - Fulton J. Sheen, Seven Words of Jesus and Mary - (New York: P.J. Kenedy & Sons, 1945).

SUFFERING OF THE INNOCENT - Fulton J. Sheen, The Rainbow of Sorrow - (New York: P.J. Kenedy & Sons 1938).

RELIGION IS A QUEST - Fulton J. Sheen, Seven Words of Jesus and Mary - (New York: P.J. Kenedy & Sons, 1945).

LUST - Fulton J. Sheen, Victory Over Vice – (New York: P.J. Kenedy & Sons, 1939).

THE HOUR - Fulton J. Sheen, Seven Words of Jesus and Mary - (New York: P.J. Kenedy & Sons, 1945).

PRUDENCE - Fulton J. Sheen, The Seven Virtues - (New York: P.J. Kenedy & Sons, 1940).

THE PURPOSE OF LIFE - Fulton J. Sheen, Seven Words of Jesus and Mary - (New York: P.J. Kenedy & Sons, 1945).

THE SELFISH - Fulton J. Sheen, Seven Words To The Cross – (New York: P.J. Kenedy & Sons, 1944).

WHEN CALVARY BECOMES THE NURSERY

(16) Fulton J. Sheen, The Seven Last Words – (New York: D. Appleton - Century Co. Ltd., Reprint Edition, 1934), pp. 23-26.

(17) Fulton J. Sheen, The Seven Virtues - (New York: P.J. Kenedy & Sons, 1940), p. 97.

(18) Fulton J. Sheen, The Rainbow of Sorrow - (New York: P.J. Kenedy & Sons 1938), pp. 107-108.

(19) Fulton J. Sheen, The Cross and The Beatitudes - (New York: P.J. Kenedy & Sons, 1937), pp. 109-110.

(20) Fulton J. Sheen, Seven Words of Jesus and Mary - (New York: P.J. Kenedy & Sons, 1944), p. 58.

(21) Fulton J. Sheen, The Seven Virtues - (New York: P.J. Kenedy & Sons, 1940), pp. 47-48.

(22) Fulton J. Sheen, The Cross and The Beatitudes - (New York: P.J. Kenedy & Sons, 1937), p. 56.

(23) Fulton J. Sheen, The Seven Virtues - (New York: P.J. Kenedy & Sons, 1940), p. 68.

(24) Fulton J. Sheen, The Rainbow of Sorrow - (New York: P.J. Kenedy & Sons 1938), p. 65.

"The Rock and the Pebble"

Pope St. John Paul II embracing Archbishop Fulton J. Sheen at St. Patrick's Cathedral in New York City on October 2, 1979 and spoke into his ear a blessing and an affirmation. He said: "You have written and spoken well of the Lord Jesus Christ. You are a loyal son of the Church"

Printed in Great Britain
by Amazon

67604926R00097